Dear Mark

We hope you enjoy
this book as much as
we do.

Warm wishes

Therese & Santi

Feb 2002.

PALACES OF GOA

HELDER CARITA

PALACES OF GOA

Models and types of Indo-Portuguese
Civil Architecture

PHOTOGRAPHY BY NICOLAS SAPIEHA

CARTAGO
LONDON

INTRODUCTION I

Architecture, like the other arts developed on territory occupied by the Portuguese, shows original characteristics which differentiate it from other «colonial» architectures.

This phenomenon is the fruit of a profound mixing of the Indian and Portuguese cultures, which the characterization *Indo-Portuguese art* conveys perfectly.

Civilian architecture in India's former Portuguese settlements still exists, in the numerous palaces and *quintas* (country estates) assembled on a tiny portion of India's vast territory. These dwellings, which, for the most part, were built not by Portuguese settlers but by Indian families of the Brahmin and Chardo castes who had converted to Christianity, are the expression of the cultural and economic heritage left to the Goans through the path they shared with the Portuguese for more than four centuries.

Behind the Oriental sensitivity of their refined façades, where the Portuguese influence is most apparent, the organisation of the interiors follows Hindu customs that the Portuguese presence never erased.

The small state of Goa, where this collection of palaces and large houses is concentrated, was in the 16th century the metropolitan zone comprising the capital of a vast maritime empire extending from Africa's east coast to the Seas of China and Japan.

Here, East and West met for the first time, and developed a dialogue nourished not only by tensions and disputes, but also of peaceful conviviality and reciprocal assimilation.

Previous page. *Detail of the entrance of the Casa dos Fernandes in Chandor*

Jealous masters of their nautical science and naval artillery, the Portuguese of the first half of the 16th century established their dominance on the Indian Ocean, thus assuring their control of nearly all the commerce between Europe and the Orient. Numerous naval battles which they led against Muslim forces, during which small numbers of Portuguese decimated far superior numbers of their opponents, conferred on the Portuguese ships a mythic aura of invincibility.

Goa and Lisbon were transformed into huge warehouses, eclipsing the splendour of Istanbul, Cairo and Venice, which had until then controlled trade in spices and many other exotic commodities.

Throughout the 16th century, Lusitanian vessels had a strong hold on the Indian Ocean, until the arrival of the first Dutch, and succeeding English fleets, which would challenge the Portuguese in the following century.

A hundred years later, European attitudes and strategies had changed. If at the beginning of the 16th century the Portuguese were still driven by a medieval vision of the crusades or by a missionary vocation, the trademarks of their presence in the East, other Europeans were carried forth by mercantile aspirations, which were served by simpler means. In the early stages of their conquest, the English were content to establish trading posts; it was only in the 19th century that they transformed all India into a colony by making it a protectorate.

In the Orient, the Portuguese dreamed of building a spiritual empire to propagate Christianity in Asia, and where Goa would be a sort of new Rome. It was that philosophy that distinguished the Portuguese from the Dutch, the English and the French, whose presence in the Indies was strictly economic and political. This fundamental difference explains the specific nature of Indo-Portuguese art forms.

In a grandiose and outsized effort, cathedrals, churches, convents and colleges were erected, not only in Goa but in other cities strategic to the empire. This constructive enthusiasm is described by Pyrard de Laval: *I am often astonished by how, in such little time, the Portuguese have managed to build so many superb structures, in churches, monasteries, palaces, fortresses and other edifices built in the European fashion.»*[1]

To the search for new markets and greater gain was added the missionary spirit, where Jesuits played a fundamental role. Some of the greatest spirits of the western clergy sojourned in these territories and left indelible traces. One such was Saint François Xavier, venerated in the Indies by Christians and Hindus alike.

In 1557, the king authorized the creation of the first superior studies at the College of Saint Paul, which became the first university in the Orient. The same year, the Jesuits installed in their Saint Paul and Rachol colleges, two printing presses which were the first in this part of the world. Under the aegis of the Jesuits, studies of the local languages Konkani and Mahratti began. Less erudite, the Franciscans founded a college of theological studies and liberal arts in the province of Bardez; there they also taught singing and music.[2] Reserved for local people, notably to the Brahmin families, this superior education created an indigenous elite that was then able to occupy an important place in the Portuguese administration of the Orient. This Indian elite made its careers not only at home, but on the east coast of Africa, in the Persian Gulf, and in Brazil.

For centuries, foreign travelers attracted by Goa's mythic reputation described a place that, through its ostentatious luxury, was characterising itself by a complex set of customs, where two worlds mixed in a manner unknown at the time. Their empire disproportionate in size to the human resources of their country, the Portuguese took to interbreeding with Indians, thereby giving rights to

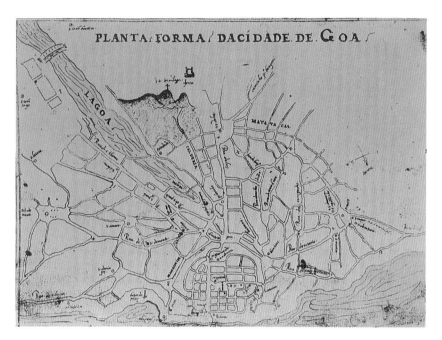

Plan of the city of Goa in Livro de Plataformas das Fortalezas da Índia, *de Manuel Godinho de Erédia, c. 1620. Royal Library, Brussels*

the local privileged classes and slowly integrating them into their own, Portuguese economic and social hierarchy.

Going beyond merely recognising the traditional rights of the Brahmins and the Chardos by allowing some of their members to participate in the imperial administration, the Portuguese also took on some behavior patterns of the local dominant classes and integrated themselves into the Hindu way of life. This adaptation of their own culture to one so far removed from Lisbon is one of the determining characteristics of Indo-Portuguese customs and art.

From domestic etiquette to the protocol for great ceremonies, Portuguese life in India obeyed complex rituals. The newcomers wanted to rival the strict customs of Hindu princes and nobles in both luxury and formality. The writings of foreigners traveling here are revelatory in describing the conventions of the day.

The Dutch traveler Jan Huyghen van Linschotten made such a reference in the early 17th century: *«The Portuguese, both half-breeds and Christians, keep their families richly and*

[1] **Pyrard de Laval**, François, *Travels to the East Indies*, Paris, 1615, vol.II, p. 42.

[2] **Souza**, Teotónio R. de, «A Cidade e o Interior no séc. XVII» in *Goa Medieval*, Editorial Estampa, 1994, p. 91.

fifty steps away, which takes her at least a quarter of an hour in getting to, because she walks so sedately and ceremoniously, holding in her hand a string of gold, pearls and precious stones.»[4]

These customs, which were often the subject of amused, if not sarcastic, descriptions by writer-voyagers, were merely Portuguese attempts to impose some social representation compatible with Eastern ways and protocols. In fact, the etiquette and practices of the Indian kingdoms' own princes and ambassadors had become very similar to those of the Portuguese community. The taste for pomp, the number of pages and armed soldiers, even the use of litters and parasols, used also by the Portuguese, were all evidence of mutual influences and gentle rivalries.

In such a context, the architecture produced by the Portuguese naturally differentiated itself from that conceived on European territory. In the same way, architecture produced later by other European settlers in Asia would also differ. As soon as the aesthetic was created, despite all its clearly Portuguese traits, it would forever be characterised by an eastern decorative taste, bequeathing a legacy of a rare and interesting cultural intercourse between two civilisations whose concepts of space and time had been profoundly different.

The palaces and the *quintas* which still survive today were for the most part built during a later period, from the second half of the 18ᵗʰ century to the beginning of the 19ᵗʰ, after Goa's golden age.

The attack on Ormuz by the Persians, with the help of the English, in 1662, and the abandonment of Malacca in 1641, after the long siege of the Dutch fleet, deprived Portugal of its maritime trade monopoly in these regions: Ormuz had controlled trade with the

magnificently. They are very respectfully served by their servants, commoners as well as nobles. They feign a majestic and poised bearing, to be all the more esteemed, and each has at least one servant who carries a veil or a cape to protect him from rain or sunshine, another who carries the sword of his master so that it does not hinder the poised smoothness of his gait.»[3]

The ritual accompanying the most insignificant outing of the viceroy or archbishop — the number of people accompanying him, his right of precedence and the magnificence of his cortège — had no comparison with practices in Europe. For example, at church, the arrival or departure of a highly-ranked lady required a ceremony which could last quite some time, according to Peyrard: *«These ladies are helped by at least one man, because they cannot walk unaided owing to the height of their clogs , often half a foot high and not well attached to their feet. ... then each one goes to her place, forty or*

[3] **Linschoten**, Jan Huyghen van, *Histoire de la navigation et de son voyage és Indes orientales*, Amsterdam, 1610.

[4] **Pyrard de Laval**, *op. cit.*, p. 168.

Jmbaſciata ſatta daſ Figſioſo deſ Re di Moxam. biqúe aſ ViceRe di Poviugaſſo iſ di 2 Agoſto 1697.

Islamic world in the Persian Gulf and Malacca had dominated exchanges with the Far East. Suddenly deprived of these two strategic facets, and incapable of simultaneously leading fronts against competing European powers and local powers of the Indian peninsula, the Portuguese empire rapidly declined.

The old city of Goa, known as the Rome of the East, or Goa Dourada (Golden Goa), had been for more than a century one of the richest and most populated cities in this part of the world. But from the middle of the 17th century, part of the noblesse and merchant class, deprived of sufficient revenue, abandoned Goa, emigrating to other cities of the empire or returning to Portugal. The legendary palaces, built by the Portuguese during the height of the city's splendour, disappeared little by little, as did the luxurious country estates which were still scattered along the banks of the Mandovi River during the 18th century.

Even though in decline, Goa and a string of territories extending from Macao to the east coast of Africa saw a resurgence of activity. The gold brought out of Brazil wasn't enough to restore the economy to its former robust state, but Goa remained a hub for commerce with Europe as the «Indies line» still posed some competition to Brazil. It was in this new context that the Christian Indian population, notably the Brahmins and the Chardos, were progressively invited to participate in the administration as full subjects of the king, receiving in exchange various privileges, titles and noble coats of arms.

The palaces and grand houses built for these indigenous families are perfect evidence of the convivial exchanges at the origin of a common culture and a shared aesthetic.

Top left. *Audience by the Viceroy to a Mozambican chief. Drawing from the Plácido Francesco Ramponi's diary, c. 1697. Priv. Coll.: Sir Bruce Ingram*
Above: *Palanquin used by Portuguese high dignitaries in India. Linschoten* 'Histoire de la Navegation, *Amsterdam, 1638. Oceanos Archive*

Civil and religious construction have left very different legacies in Portuguese India. While religious architecture is characterised by a large number of monuments erected from the second half of the 16th century to the middle of the 17th century, the empire's golden era. Civil architecture, now seen mainly in the large palaces of the second half of the 18th century and early 19th century, bear witness to a later period, that of the empire's decline. The palaces and country estates of the prosperous period have almost all disappeared, as has the entire city of Goa, save a few magnificent churches and convents.

It was the sacred nature of the religious edifices which spared them from destruction, as the local Christianised populations were determined to protect them. The region's monsoons, with their torrential rains, heat and clawing humidity, could ruin a building in only a few years, and its rapid transformation into a tropical wilderness. By contrast, the religious patrimony of the 18th and 19th centuries is modest and of little aesthetic value, compared to the formal magnificence of the grand houses constructed during this later period.

Civil architecture, developed over a much longer period, encountered several waves of complex and profound aesthetic and cultural influence which correspond to two distinct cycles. The first, which coincides with the great phase of religious architecture, stems from a colonial aesthetic, developed by Portuguese settlers in India. By the time of the second cycle, with the slow decline of the empire and the corresponding ebb in the power of the church, a civil architecture was being born in which Hindu aesthetic norms asserted themselves with more authority.

During the first period, in both civil and religious domains, the spaciousness of the

Above. Church of Espirito Santo in Margão at the end of the 19th century. Paul and De Sousa Archives. Pangim

Left. Detail of the side door of the Church of São Paulo in Diu. Photo H. C.

11

buildings was primarily Portuguese and European, while the Indian culture showed itself in small touches in form and decoration, highlighted here and there with irreverence by local symbols.

During the second period, the interior spatial structures took on the traditional models of Hindu domestic architecture.

It is important to distinguish between these two cycles, which don't appear clearly in religious buildings, in order to understand this architecture and the whole cultural process which developed in Goa during more than four centuries.

To identify them more easily, we will refer to civil architecture built during the first cycle by Portuguese colonists as «colonial architecture.» We will call the civil architecture built by Brahmins and Chardos «Indo-Portuguese,»

even if both styles deserve that title, though in different intensities.

As we have already explained, the Portuguese recognition of the castes' rights and customs gave birth to new social stratification, distinguishing the converted Brahmins and Chardos in India's class system. During the decline of the colonial empire, these castes, who by now occupied many of the key administrative posts, began to profit from the political and economic situation by developing trade with Brazil and Europe, most notably during Napoleon's blockade on English ships and during the Opium War in China.

It is by keeping this socio-economic context in mind that we can understand the evolution of Goan architecture, and notably the luxury and magnificence that flourished in 18ᵗʰ and

Left. *Church and College
of São Paulo in Diu.
Photo. H. C.*

19th century houses even as Portuguese power was waning in the East.

Despite the difficulty imposed by the rarity of preserved structures of the first cycle, it is important to study it, too, to understand the evolution and the aesthetic significance of Goa's architectural patrimony.

It is only by studying the first cycle, where different aesthetic currents mingled, that we can understand the continuity of formal and ornamental programmes that, even as they disappeared during the 18th and 19th centuries, would become the foundation values of Indo-Portuguese architecture.

Above. *Detail of the main
façade of the Church of São
Paulo in Diu. Photo. H. C.*

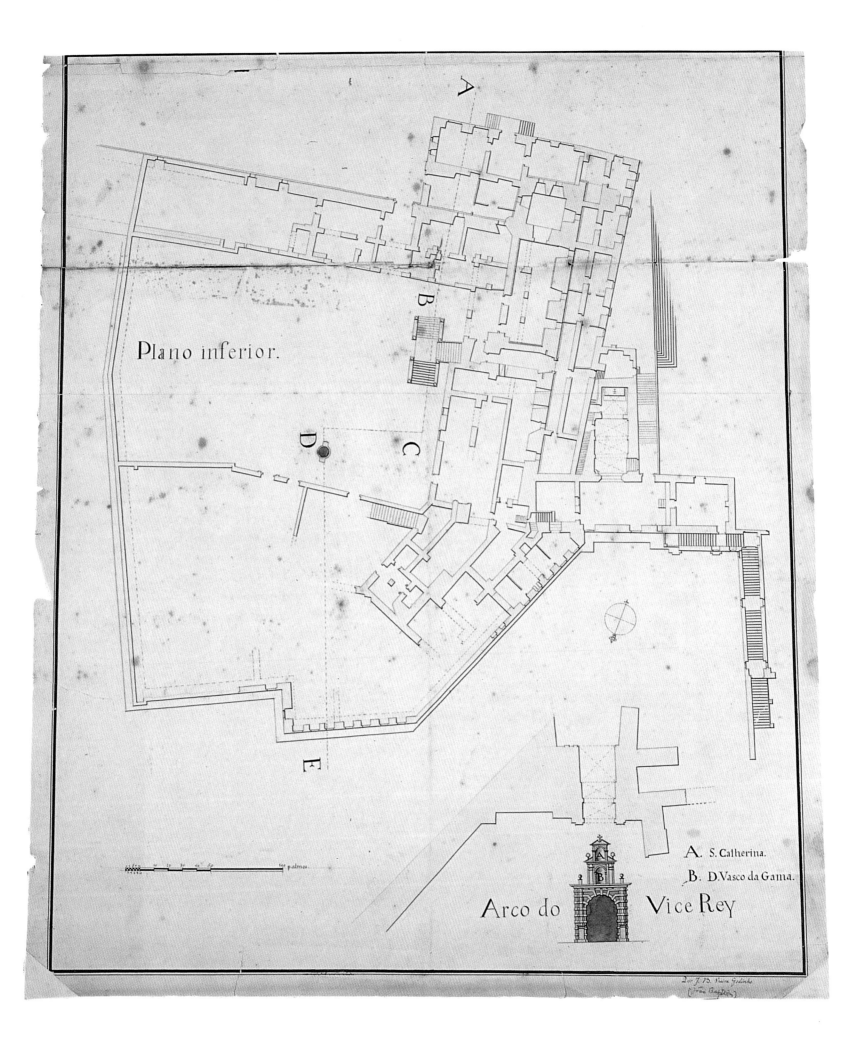

Plano inferior.

A. S. Catherina.

B. D. Vasco da Gama.

Arco do Vice Rey

«CHÃ» ARCHITECTURE II

AND THE FIRST AESTHETIC MODEL FOR THE PALACES OF GOA

The first products of Portuguese civil architecture in India are imbued with the tendancy found in Portuguese fortresses of the 16th century, called «chã» (plane) in Portugal. Intimately linked to military architecture, the «chã» style was distancing itself from the international aesthetic of the day, Italian mannerism, and developing its own, highly original style in Portugal and its colonies.

Defined for the first time by George Kubler in *Portuguese Plane Architecture*, the «chã» fashion, which lasted from the late 16th century to the early 18th century, was characterised by great functionality and a preference for constructive aspects rather than decoration. Its conception, realised above all by military engineers, it integrated the classic principles of the Renaissance, and thereby conferred on buildings an impressive rigor and austerity.

Supreme in maritime and military domains, the Portuguese were nonetheless constantly confronted by the lack of human resources and by a constant state of war. Their civil architecture was steeped in a vocabulary of power: its aesthetic conveyed calm, solid and imposing strength.

For this small population confronted by the immensity of its empire, this aesthetic was an absolute necessity. If the decorative drought in this architecture evokes the style inspired by the Counter-Reform, the accentuation of architectonic volumes clearly tries to demonstrate an image of permanence to peoples recently subdued. It was no accident that the

Previous page. *Plan of the Palácio da Fortaleza of the Viceroys in Goa. Survey carried out during the second half of the 18th century. Library of the Sociedade de Geografia*

15

residence of the viceroys was called Palácio da Fortaleza (Palace of the Fortress), and that it never renounced, over the course of centuries, despite the magnificence of its interiors, its martial façade.

Among the oldest examples still visible of this architecture is the Palácio dos Arcebispos (Palace of the Archbishops), built in the 16th century.

The Palace of the Fortress dates from the same period. It was demolished in the 19th century, but had been inventoried in the 18th century, which allows us to have an idea of its architecture.[5] In both cases, the choice of the «chã» model, with its simple and massive volumes, is clear. The essentially utilitarian and functional spirit which inspired all this architecture, justifies its organisation into several, independent spaces. Tall, steeply inclined roofs hung over each room, giving an external appearance of height. The ground floor, with its few windows, reinforced the buildings' sense of solidity and strength.

The palace called *Casa da Pólvora*, ordered by the viceroy Dom Francisco da Gama at the end of the 16th century, is another example of a princely residence. On the banks of the Mandovi, this palace, surrounded by gardens, had the advantage of being set apart from the numerous secretariats and public offices which surrounded the Palace of the Fortress. Destroyed in the 19th century, this palace is well represented in the early 19th century paintings of Goa in the collection of Alpoim Galvão; his map, dating from the 18th century, is held in the library at Ajuda. The same «chã» characteristics of austerity and formal simplicity emerge here too, even though we can detect in the houses and gardens along the Mandovi's banks the temptation of the charms and furnishings appropriate to a country *quinta*.

From the descriptions of several travelers, the cold style of this palace was that of the palaces and houses in the city. Speaking of Goa in 1623, Pietro della Valle noted that «*the buildings are very plain and without ornament.*»[6] This simplicity in the decoration of façades did not prevent Tavernier from affirming, during his stay in Goa in 1641, that «*the houses are for the most part superbly built, and particularly the palace of the viceroy.*»[7]

Barely decorated, these edifices had a simple, clear form, the porch or entry awning being the only distinctive element. It brought a gracious tone to the frigidity of the ensemble. The imposing volumes, their orientation, the rare windows encased in sobre and straight frames, carried the language and image of power.

Below. *View of the Palácio Real de Santos in the 16th century. Detail of the illumination by Simon de Bening in* Geneologia dos Reis de Portugal. *British Museum Library, London*

[5] These inventories are now dispersed. The inventory of the viceroy's Palace of the Fortress is preserved in the library of the Geographical Society of Lisbon. That of the Palace of the Inquisition is in the Gabinete de Estudos Arqueológicos de Engenharia Militar.

[6] **Valle**, Pietro della, *The Travels of … in India.* Asian Educational Services, New Delhi, 1991, p. 155.

[7] **Tavernier**, Jean-Baptiste, *The six voyages of …*, Paris, 1676. II, p. 128.

Even though it cannot be considered an original element, the colonnaded porch with a stairway leading to the first floor took on particular importance in Goa. Even though its usage and significance changed over time, it became a defining element of Indo-Portuguese architecture. In colonial Portuguese architecture, it was used primarily as a means for illustrating the policy of global power and social dominance developed by the Portuguese. The viceroy placed his guards, outfitted in blue livery and halberds along the stairs. The nobility, and even the archbishop, imitated the viceroy's practices to the finest detail, with the number of their servants and the luxury of their presentation. Moreover, the Portuguese

Above and left. *Casa dos Peres in São Pedro and detail of the entrance door of the Palácio dos Viscondes de Ribandar in Ribandar. Author's drawings*

17

Above. *View of the façade over the gardens of the Palácio dos Arcebispos in Goa at the end of the 19th century. Paul and De Sousa Archives. Pangim*

Right. *Detail of the entrance porch of the Palácio dos Arcebispos in Goa*

were not the only ones to be impressed by such imposing shows. Tavernier remarked during his visit to Goa that *«one even sees blacks followed by thirty superbly dressed slaves!»*[8]

This austere and dry architecture belied the wish to construct a way of life adapted to Hindu concepts of social stratification, and could rival the luxury and magnificence of the Indian kings and princes whom the Portuguese were courting through their respective ambassadors.

That is how the Palace of the Archbishops still appears to us today. The access to the first floor is assured by an exterior staircase housed in a covered porch, in the style of Portuguese 16th century palaces. The main façade, also typical of «chá» architecture, was formerly protected by a walled courtyard which no longer exists but which is still visible in the photographs taken in the last century by Paul and De Sousa. As in this palace, the only distinctive element of the façade of the viceroy's palace-fortress was the exterior stairway protected by a porch with Tuscan columns, opening onto a walled courtyard, known in those days as the Terreiro do Sabaio.

The self-sufficiency of these palace-fortresses within the urban fabric of the city gave them an archaic image akin to late Gothic. Enclosed within a walled courtyard, their floor plans reveal a vision of a discontinued but highly hierarchic internal structure.

The palace of the kings of Sundém in Pondá, built in the 18th century, even though later is another example providing references to «chá» architecture and the Portuguese colonial model. Its almost archaic character is due to the fact that the kings of Sundém wanted to appropriate an aesthetic which was imposed in Portuguese India as the model of power.

---

[8] **Tavernier**, *ibid.*, p. 130.

Recently remodeled, notably on one of its principal façades, the palace still consists of a long structure over the gardens, the first floor resembling that of the Palácio dos Arcebispos, with its straight, unornamented window frames, in the purest «chã» tradition.

Likewise, two palaces still found today at São Pedro and at Ribandar display the same characteristics: the house of the Peres family and the former palace of the Viscounts of Ribandar. The latter, profoundly altered at the level of the balconied windows, still has its stone door framed by Tuscan columns and crowned by a pediment of classical design. In both cases, the buildings were developed in a long, rectangular block, with unornamented, rectilinear windows and a façade without pilasters. In this way, both give an impression of great austerity.

Lacking the symbolic charge of the viceroy's and archbishop's palaces which truly were fortified palaces, these buildings exhibit an elegant urbanism that developed after the initial, militarily-driven period of Portuguese occupation. This new civilian taste was subsequently developed along the Mandovi River, affirming itself as an aesthetic value during the Mannerist period, while the earlier policy of force gave way to a subtler policy reflecting power through formal display.

Above and left.
Detail of the main façade and entrance porch of the Palácio dos Arcebispos in Goa

19

Left. *Palácio dos Reis de Súndem complex in Bandorános at the end of the 19ʰ century. Paul and De Sousa Archives. Pangim*
Above. *Detail of the main floor balcony*

II-1 THE VICEROY'S PALACE OF THE FORTRESS IN GOA

For more than three centuries, this was the palace *par excellence* of the viceroys. Forming an integral part of the colonials' administrative infrastructures, the palace opened up onto several buildings around a square called, as in Lisbon, the Terreiro do Paço. Contrary to Lisbon, where the plaza borders the Tagus River, this square was situated so as to face the center of the city. Seen from the river, the palace presented a fortified façade hanging over an esplanade bordering the Mandovi which was called the Caes do Vice-Rei, or the Viceroy's Quay. This façade was incorporated into the old city walls, and the two squares were connected by the Arco dos Vice-Reis (Archway of the Viceroys), which is all that is left today of this vast ensemble. As mentioned earlier, this palace was, by its architectural and urban aesthetic, similar to the royal palaces of the late Gothic. This group of buildings, quite independent from the city and having no

Detail of the area where the Palácio dos Vice-Reis was situated in Goa at the end of the 16ᵗʰ century, in Jan Linschoten, Histoire de la Navigation... *Amsterdam, 1638*

contact with the Mandovi apart from the views from its balconies and verandas, more closely resembled the royal palace in Sintra or the Alcáçovas Palace in Lisbon than to the Paço da Ribeira on the Tagus River.

Normally known as the Palácio da Fortaleza, the building was part of Goa's ancient fortress, the Ádil Sahah, and leaned up against the city walls. After his Portuguese troops conquered the city in 1510, Afonso de Albuquerque had the fort restored, and the city's first commander-in-chief, Rodrigo Rebelo,[9] made his quarters here.

In 1554, Dom Pedro de Mascarenhas chose it as his residence. It had become painful for him to climb the grand stairway of the Sabaio palace[10], which had been the viceroys' residence for the first half of the 16ᵗʰ century.

The palace's location next to the river, with a view over the estuary, made it was more similar to that of the royal palace in Lisbon, the Paço Real da Ribeira, a comparison which doubtless encouraged the viceroys to move in and to make this building their official palace.

From an architectural point of view, the palace was constructed of a series of spaces that grew organically from one another. The edifice took on a sumptuous character, described by several travelers, more by reason of its scale and its proportions than by its elaborate lines.

[9] **Correia**, Gaspar, *Lendas da Índia*, Lisbon, 1858-64, vol. II, pp. 158-176.
[10] **Couto**, Diogo do, *Décadas*, Lisbon, 1977-1988. Vol. II, book I, ch. 3.

Planta do Pallacio da Fortaleza, em que rezidiraõ todos os Governadores, e Vice-Reys, em quanto se naõ despovuou a Cidade.

Especado pela direçaõ da linha A B C D E.

A survey taken in 1779 gives us a detailed description of its appearance. The design showed the influence of «chã» plane architecture and an organisational order which rejects Renaissance composition.

Of all the descriptions of the palace, the one written by Pyrard de Laval gives us the surest details. He also described the viceroy's quay in 1608. *«It is some seven hundred paces long and two hundred wide, straight, flat, and bordered on the river side by a handsome wall with stone steps. It is closed on one side by the walls of the viceroy's palace and the city, and on the other by those of other squares. This square or quay, which they call Terreiro, usually serves as an access to all the trading vessels of Indian merchants which berth here, as much because of the fortress as because of the viceroy, who from his window or balcony can see everything that arrives there and what goes on; the square is always full of vessels and of infinite numbers of people. There is a very fine building, in the form of the Place Royal in Paris...»*[11]

The similarity between these two edifices in Pyrard's eye can be explained by the Mannerist design of the façade, with arcades at ground level and an Indo-Portuguese roof line, which in its traditional French «scissor» form resembled the roof line of the former Place Royal, today the Place des Vosges.

On the Terreiro do Paço also stood another palace, the Paço da Relação, where legal matters were judged. To the right of the viceroy's palace was situated the Cadeia do Tronco prison, and to the left, the royal armory, both forming an integral part of the palace.

Pyrard gave the following description: *«as to the fortress or the viceroy's palace, it is sump-*

---

[11] **Pyrard de Laval**, *op. cit.*, p. 75.

Above. *Side elevation of the Palácio da Fortaleza dos Vice-Reis da Índia. Survey carried out during the second half of the 18th century. Library of the Sociedade de Geografia de Lisboa*

23

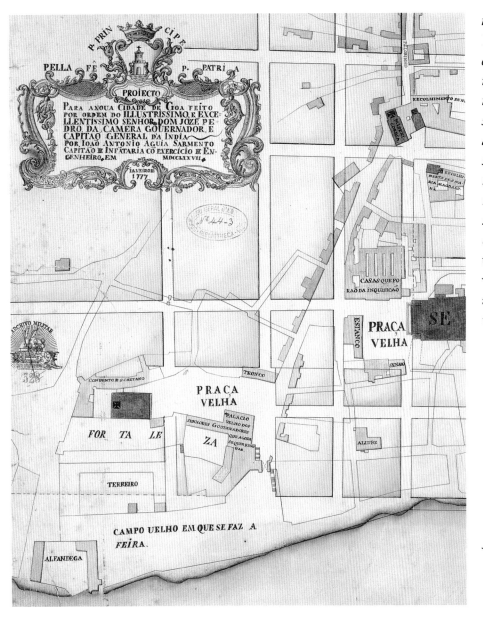

Detail of the project for the renovation of the city of Goa dated 1777, showing the location of the Palácio dos Vice-Reis within the layout of the old city.
Gabinete de Estudos Históricos de Fortificação e Obras Militares.
Photos P.C. and C.C.

they call Câmara Presidial [Paço da Relação]... *This viceroy's palace is not big enough to hold the city's artillery, but it has good and comfortable rooms. On entering, one finds to one's right hand the prison they call Tronco, which is part of the said palace; to the left are the stores and the king's arsenal. This palace is equipped with all necessities, church, clock tower, water, even the king's treasury is there in part, the other part of it being in the Franciscan convent. There are two handsome courtyards, and it is possible to walk from one into the other.»* (These two courtyards are the viceroy's quay and the Terreiro do Paço, which communicate through the viceroy's arch; the stairway to which Pyrard refers is in the Terreiro do Paço.) *«In the first courtyard, to the left, there is a very wide staircase built of stone which leads to a large room where are represented in painting all the fleets and vessels which sailed to the Indies, with their number, date, and captain's name, and even those ships that were wrecked en route are portrayed. It is a hideous thing to see so many lost ships. In short, there is not the smallest vessel come from Portugal which is not portrayed here, along with its name, its history and its encounters. Further along one finds another, larger room which is that of the viceroy and the nobility; and there sits the Council. There are painted in full-length all the viceroys who have been in India. No one may enter this room, as it is surrounded by guards. The palace is on a high point of land, and it is very strong on its river side, with strong, high walls; it is the prettiest view of all the city.»*[12]

Tavernier, who stayed in Goa in 1641 and again in 1648, visited the palace but never reached the viceroy's audience hall. The painted armadas were still in the first large room. *«Most of the houses are superbly built, and particularly the viceroy's palace. There are*

tuously constructed: and above all there is a great square on the town side which they call Campo *(Terreiro do Paço, where nobles and courtesans are to be found, as many on foot as in litter chairs. Because the viceroy never comes out without having had the drums beaten the day before; so that all the nobility is alerted to come on horseback in the early hours of the morning, and they all wait there until he appears, everyone beautifully dressed and in orderly fashion. In front of the door of the viceroy's palace there is a large building where the parliament sits, which*

---

[12] **Pyrard de Laval**, *ibid.*, pp. 77-79.

24

numerous apartments, and in one section of the very largest rooms, one sees many paintings representing the ships that have come from Lisbon, with the name of the vessel and that of its captain, as well as the quantity of artillery pieces mounted on it.»[13]

According to a letter from Dom Francisco da Gama, it was Diogo do Couto who restored the paintings that Tavernier saw: «*The armada panels that were in this house were all badly damaged and had been removed. For three years I argued to persuade the viceroy to have them restored, and finally I was able to convince him. He therefore assigned me the task, and in one month I had already had more than one hundred panels done, with beautiful colors, by the painter Godinho...*»[14]

Pyrard's description and the palace floor plan give us a vision of the building's architecture, composed of a succession of volumes.

In 1685, an epidemic devastating the city forced the Count of Vila Verde to abandon the city and set up residence in the palace called *Casa da Pólvora* at Panelim, on the outskirts of Goa. In succeeding years, while the Palace of the Viceroy was no longer the ruler's residence, the audience hall continued to be used for official receptions. During his visit to Goa in 1812, Cottineau de Kloguen[15] referred to the palace shortly before it was destroyed, in 1820.

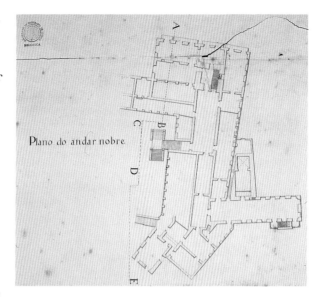

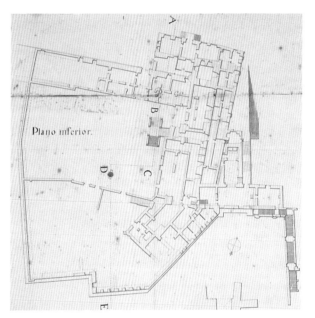

Left. *Plans of the ground and main floor of the Palácio da Fortaleza dos Vice-Reis da Índia during the second half of the 18th century. Library of the Sociedade de Geografia de Lisboa*

[13] **Tavernier**, *op. cit.*, p. 128.

[14] **Aragão**, A. C. Teixeira de, *Descrição Geral e Histórica das Moedas Cunhadas em Nome dos Reis, Regentes e Governadores de Portugal*. Lisbon, 1880 (Oporto, 1966), vol. III, p. 42.

[15] **Kloguen**, Rev. Denis Cottineau de, *An Historical Sketch of Goa*, Madras, 1831.

II-2   THE ARCHBISHOP'S PALACE IN GOA

Above. *Detail of the balconied window of the main floor of the Palácio dos Arcebispos in Goa clearly showing the strictness and simplicity of lines in plane architectural aesthetics.*
Photo H. C.

Although it lacks the imposing character of the palaces of the Fortress or of the Inquisition, this building has the merit of being the only civil edifice of Goa's golden age to remain for us today.

Its construction began at the end of the 16th century, at the same time as that of the cathedral, which communicated directly with it. Seen from the river, this building has the scale of a fortified palace, like that of the viceroys.

In 1608, Pyrard noted that the palace's construction was finished but that the cathedral was still in progress. At the time, the archdiocese of Goa was directed by Dom Aleixo de Meneses. It was under this archbishop that the palace was fully realised, and we find on the entry stairs and in the living rooms the double-headed eagle, symbol of the Augustinian Order, to which archbishop Dom Aleixo belonged.

Several aspects of this palace show affinities with the palace of the Fortress. Both had their entries on the city side of the building, which created a porch and large staircase opening onto the square. In both palaces, the rear walls abutted the Mandovi's banks. An old photograph taken from the river by Paul and De Sousa shows the palace composed of several groups of buildings with columned verandas similar to those that Pyrard mentioned when describing the palace of the Fortress: «*The viceroy, from a window or a gallery, can see all that arrive and that pass by.*»[16]

Although it is in a dilapidated condition today, the palace's entry court, which once was closed in, presents an austere design for the palace's principal building. Its windows are cased in straight frames devoid of ornament. The two porches which lead to the two ends of the main building were apparently built at different times. If the main porch exhibits the «chã» principles of the initial building project, the second porch was built or altered during the 18th century. The later works must have coincided with the transformation of the great audience hall into a chapel after the departure of the archbishops for the palace at Panelim, their new official residence at the end of the 17th century.

Inside, the building is organised around two vast rooms which correspond to the antechamber and audience hall.

One can still see today, under their roofs, the wooden chevrons sculpted after the Indian fashion and which can be found in other important dwellings up until the 18th century. At the time, ceilings would have been painted as they were in churches, but here the frescoes have disappeared with the building's disuse. As in the viceroy's palace, the audience hall was decorated with portraits. The portraits were carried to Panelim when the archbishops moved residence. Cottineau de Kloguen, who

---

[16] **Pyrard de Laval**, *op. cit.*, p. 41.

stayed at Panelim at the archbishop's invitation, wrote that «*the ante-chamber contains the life-sized paintings of all the archbishops of Goa until the present one.*»[17]

Above. *Façade of the Palácio dos Arcebispos in Goa. It is still possible to observe the ventilating tiles for the inner rooms*

[17] **Kloguen**, Rev. Denis Cottineau de, *op. cit.*, p. 106.

II-3 THE PALACE OF THE «CASA DA PÓLVORA»

Above. *The Palácio da Casa da Pólvora. Engraving from the Lopes Mendes' book,* Índia Portuguesa

Opposite. *The Palácio da Casa da Pólvora which functioned as the Hospital Real Militar. Detail from a painting of the latter half of the 18th century. Alpoim Galvão Collection. Plan of the same palace with indications for its conversion into a hospital. Library of the Palácio Nacional da Ajuda, Lisbon*

Through its aesthetic nature, this palace exhibits all the values of «chã» architecture. Nonetheless, its location and its country setting correspond to the Mannerist cycle we will present later on. We know of a floor plan for this palace dating to the 18th century and of two depictions of it which give us a good idea of its conception and its aesthetic.

According to an inscription found on the front door, the palace was built by Dom Francisco da Gama, who governed from 1597 to 1600. *«During the reign in Portugal of the Catholic King Dom Filipe III, the city had this Powder House (Casa da Pólvora) built from money at one percent. Francisco da Gama, count and admiral, being viceroy of this state, completed and perfected this house, where the viceroy Dom Miguel de Noronha, Count of Linhares, currently resides in the year 1630.»*[18]

The inscription does not specify whether Dom Francisco also had the palace built. The fact that the inscription was ordered by the Count of Linhares indicates that the viceroy had at least undertaken improvements and he may well have been the builder of the palace which stood next to the Casa da Pólvora (Powder House), from which the palace takes its name. Neither Pyrard, who was in Goa from 1608 to 1610, and Della Valle, here in 1623, speak yet of this residence. A few years later, Tavernier, visiting Goa in 1648, said that the viceroy Dom Filipe de Mascarenhas used this palace as a leisure residence: *«five or six times he sent me a gentleman to take me to the Powder House outside of town where he was very often.»*[19], which seems to confirm that the palace was run by the Count of Linhares.

Like the palaces of the Fortress and the archbishops, this construction shows «chã» characteristics: organic development and great economy of decoration. The main portal, which is the only remarkable element of the façade, has a more detailed design, in contrast to the simple rectangular window frames above the balconies.

The palace floor plan shows a large interior staircase of baroque inspiration on two levels, which suggests alterations to the palace when it became the official residence of the viceroys.

[18] **Fonseca**, José Nicolau, *Sketch of the City of Goa*, New Delhi, 1986, p. 326.

[19] **Tavernier**, *op. cit.*, p. 138.

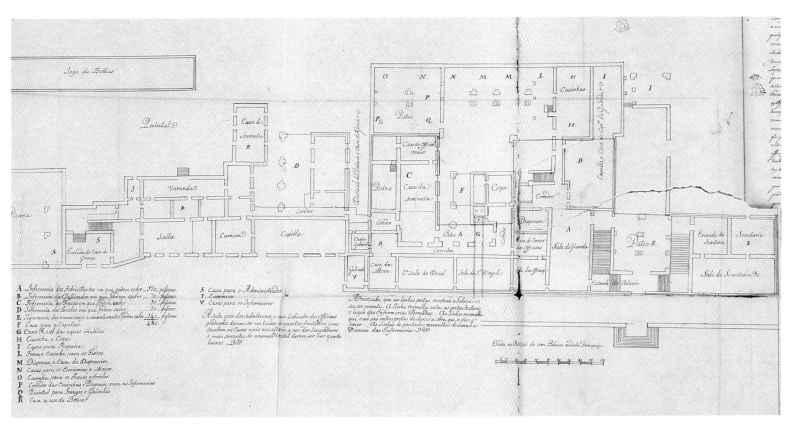

HOSPITAL REAL MILITAR

Mannerism of Italian Influence III

IN THE 17TH CENTURY
COUNTRY ESTATES OF «GOLDEN GOA»

P arallel to the development of plane architecture, we find in Goa the emergence of a Mannerist movement from the end of the 16th century to the 17th century, with distinctly Italian influences. This style was considerably different from the contemporary architecture in Portugal itself. This stylistic influence was clearly linked to the economic supremacy of the Church and the Company of Jesus. It was introduced while the Portuguese empire was still wealthy, between the peace signed with the Sultan of Bijapur in 1580 and the fall of Ormuz in 1622.

The Mannerist examples which have survived are even more rare than those of the «chā» period, despite the fact that this was the era during which the most significant religious buildings were erected.

It is this style, of which most examples have disappeared, that can explain the permanence of the Italian Mannerist influence on Indo--Portuguese civil architecture during the 18th

Above. *Detail of the façade of the Seminário do Chorão, Church emphasizing architectural features identical to those from civil architecture*

Opposite. *Detail from the painting of the second half of the 18th century showing a country estate whose design shows mannerist influence. Alpoim Galvão Collection*

DAUGIM

Above. *Narthex of the Nossa Senhora da Penha de França Church in Britona*

century, and which is without equal in Portugal's own architecture.

With the exception of the Palácio da Inquisição (Palace of the Inquisition), this Mannerist school is mainly expressed in civil architecture, palaces and country houses, built by the Portuguese nobility on the banks of the Mandovi.

The change from the Islamic city violently conquered by Albuquerque to the new, Portuguese-occupied Goa brought no great ruptures. The new arrivals retained and simply transformed the older edifices in this city, which was already imposing when they arrived. It was, in fact, avowedly difficult to reformulate the structure of Goa, as the Portuguese had done in other cities like Daman or Bassein.

Because Goa's urban plan had Islamic origins, it had few boulevards or large circulation axes; the main traffic axis in the city was the Mandovi River. The biggest buildings tended, therefore, to be found along the river banks. The discourse of power, linked early on to an imposing image of a fortified city, evolved into one of formal grandeur, expressing itself to greatest advantage in a highly politicised urban decor.

Alongside these public buildings, members of the nobility and wealthy merchants installed their own houses in privileged venues, thereby contributing to the architectural richness of the *Rome of the East* dreamed of by Goa's founders.

Even after the decline and ruin of the old city of Goa, these *quintas* and palaces would be praised by foreigners who travelled here. Dellon described Goa in 1673-76 this way: «... *the river banks are embellished by the noble structures of churches, castles and palaces... Their houses are large and their gardens magnificent, full of trees that flower all year long, of leaves, and of fruit. Pangim, which is at a distance of one league from the city, is a large village or Aldea, which surpasses many cities in beauty; it is the place where people of quality have summer palaces to which they can escape during the hot season. The gardens are in proportion to the beauty of the houses, and all are to be admired...*»[20]

Of his visits to Goa between 1692 and 1704, Hamilton reported: «*The banks of the river are beautified with noble structures of churches, castles*

[20] **Dellon**, Charles, *Nouvelle relation d'un voyage fait aux Indes Orientales*, Amsterdam, 1699, p. 202.

Left. View over the banks of the Mandovi River from the Casa dos Colaço in Ribandar. Although it was altered in the 19th century, the tripartite design of the façade is still evident from other cases of the 16th and 17th centuries

and gentlemen houses... Their houses are large, and their outsides magnificent...» [21]

Arrayed along the Mandovi's banks, the palaces not only created an architectural ensemble of great formal impact, but it also helped develop an original aesthetic, which might explain how the Mannerist tradition lasted in civil architecture throughout the 18th and 19th centuries.

If Della Valle wrote that the buildings of Goa were very simple and undecorated – an explicit reference to plane architecture – the Abbot Carré affirmed, on the subject of the farms along the Mandovi: *«The outskirts are lovely and pleasant... there are also some country houses, but only decorated on their façades...as their incomes diminish every day.»*[22]

In 1672, the date of Abbot Carré's visit to Goa, the city was already in full decline, which explains his descriptions of houses being well-finished only on their exteriors. This reference to decorated façades, made by a cultured and well-travelled clergyman on diplomatic mission to Goa, is significant. Abraham Parson[23], who passed through Goa in 1776, also sang the praises of the *quintas*. He remarked that they were built according to European style. They must therefore have been conceived with European tastes, far removed from the «chã» model used for most of the palaces in town.

The aesthetic purposes of these houses, built for leisure and ostentation, differed from those which were at the origin of the great urban palaces of Goa. Their values, clearly linked to the earlier policy of displaying power through giving an impression of strength and austerity, lost their pertinence in this new environment of gardens and palm groves.

If the drawings of Lopes Mendes are not very precise, they nonetheless give us the general spatial elements which prove that architecture was moving away from the «chã» criteria.

Likewise, the paintings of Goa landscapes in the collection of Alpoim Galvão give details which enable us to see this evolution.

Above. Central body of the façade showing the central docking entrance for the owner's skiff. Library of the Pangim Archive

---

[21] **Hamilton**, Captain Alexander, *A new account of the East Indies*, London, 1744, vol. I, p. 249.

[22] **Carré**, Abbé, *The Travels of ... in India and the Near East 1672 to 1674*, New Delhi, Asian Educational Services, 1990, vol. I, p. 217.

[23] **Parson**, Abraham, *Travels in India*, London, 1808, p. 242.

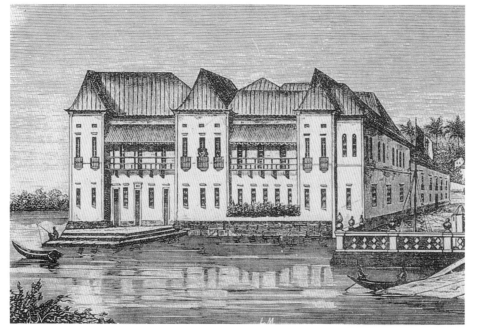

The model is perfectly recognisable in existing documents. One can see the role of decoration as well as the Mannerist inspiration in both the design and composition of façades.

The iconography presents examples in which we recognise a classically-inspired tripartite façade model. This model can be seen in the Palace of the Inquisition with its three large portals. The palace of the governor of Daman is composed of three parts linked by two verandas. This latter can be seen in Lopes Mendes' drawing of the palace at Pangim, before 19th and 20th century construction profoundly altered its appearance.

The Casa dos Perez (House of the Fathers) in Ribandar, even though modified in the 19th century, has kept the same type of architecture. In this case, it is the two verandas which are important, still placed along the same format with three small, turreted buildings.

There are a few houses built along classical and conventional lines in which we can detect a clear articulation between the ground floor and the first floor. Examples include the Casa dos Proença in Calangute, the Casa dos Monteiro in Candolim, and the Casa dos Costa in Majorda. These will be described in more detail in the chapter on the first cycle of civil architecture built by the Brahmin and Chardo families.

It is by looking at details that we may detect the Italian Mannerist characteristics which have no equivalent in Lisbon's architecture. The alternating pilasters and windows with Corinthian motifs, which only became fashionable in Portugal during the Baroque period of Dom João V, are typical of the façades of these palaces. The triangular pediments above the balcony windows on the first floor are also a constant element of the Mannerist style. Although this type of design was not completely unknown in Portugal, it was only visible in exceptional and particularly erudite examples, such as the former Ribeira royal

palace or the palace of the Dukes of Bragance at Vila Viçosa.

These decorative elements are the fruit of interaction between civil and religious architectures. Religious architecture also harbors the same ornamental models and plastic concepts.

The *quinta* built in Neura by the Augustine fathers, which is still preserved, is an example of this period. In 1695, during his visit to Goa, Gemelli Carreri visited the house: *«After dinner, we went to see the large palm grove of the Augustinians, where one father had built a very tasteful house, complete with lovely furniture...»*[24] Slightly modified, the *quinta* has kept a magnificent front door elegantly framed by pilasters and crowned by the coat of arms of the Augustine order. The façade is composed of a series of alternating windows and pilasters.

The affinities with religious architecture stemmed naturally from the incontestable power of the church in Goa, and particularly that of the Jesuit priests who had had their aesthetic training in Portugal and in Rome.

The great erudition of the priests of the Company of Jesus, as well as their active participation in the city's social life, led them to work like architects in several domains, even

to the point of intervening in urban planning, where their work had even more impact than that of the architects and military engineers imported from Lisbon. Above all, they ordered the construction of the fortresses on the coast of Malabar.

If we owe the «chã» aesthetic to the first masters of military architecture, it is to the Jesuits that we owe the spread of the Mannerist aesthetic which came directly from Rome. The Jesuits substituted the policy of military power for a more subtle one based on the value of the word and Aristotelian rhetoric. Having its

---

[24] **Carreri**, Gemelli, *Giro delle Mondo*, Venice, 1719, p. 186.

and civil architectural projects. The supporting structures for the verandas and balconies are proof of this. Planned along the model of upper galleries in church naves, these supports took the form of three small corbels, as in the churches in Lisbon; these elements had until now been absent in civil architecture. The same interaction can be found in the ogees and the eaves. Projecting far beyond the walls to protect them from monsoons, the roofs stretched out in a succession of frames whose design was repeated both in churches and in private houses. In some cases, such as in one of the houses of the Monteiro family in

Above and right. Although it is the only building to have survived to the present day from the vast number of luxurious country estates belonging to the Church in Goa, its mannerist concept in design such as the great entrance gate is an example of the interinfluence between religious and civil architecture. The old Agostinho friars country estate in Verem

roots in the conclusions of the Council of Trent, this discourse puts greater value on the visual context and the progressive vocation towards greater luxury in urban and architectural decor. From the earliest examples of the 16th century, which displayed a certain austere grandeur, as witnessed in the Sé Catedral (cathedral) or the Igreja dos Agostinhos (church of the Augustinians), religious architecture tended to develop its Mannerist grammar in a profusion of decoration. Goa, with its status as the «new Rome» in the East, was no stranger to the ideology of the church and of the Jesuit fathers.

With its legendary economic resources, the Church of Goa was the city's most powerful patron. Commissioning numerous works, it also trained artisans, builders and architects. In the beginning of the 17th century, the plan and the work on the convent of Notre Dame du Pilier was entrusted to Brother Manuel Batista[25], an Indian born in Daman.

The decorative elements and all the finishing of the details reveal that both drawings and craftsmen were liberally exchanged on religious

Candolim, the windows borders are framed by angels, above whom flies the dove of the Holy Spirit; motifs that would be much more suitable for a chapel than for a domestic dwelling.

Only the *quintas* of the Augustinians of Neura and the Monteiro family in Candolim, along with the Dean's palace at Quepém, which itself has the rather late date of the end of the 18th century, are still preserved today with few alterations. As a result, the Mannerist

---

[25] **Sousa Viterbo**, *Dicionário Histórico e Documental dos Arquitectos…*, Imprensa Nacional, vol. 1, p. 87.

influence on the period is best seen in the drawings of Lopes Mendes, various 19th century photographs, and the paintings of Goa in the Alpoim Galvão collection. The collective vision given by these documents allows us to situate old details on buildings that have been since remodeled, such as the houses of the Machado family in Nagoa, the Pinto family in Santa Cruz or the Alemão family in Betalbatim, where one discovers elements that only be understood as stemming from a well-founded aesthetic current.

In the Casa dos Monteiros in Candolim, which we will present later as an example of

Brahmin architecture, the tympanum of the pediment crowning the windows is graced with busts of the purest classical tradition. The Italian influence here is clear and direct.

The country house-palace of the archbishops in Panelim, which has also disappeared[26], is known to us thanks to a drawing of the plan and to a 19th century photograph from the albums of Paul and De Sousa. The palace had been restored by Archbishop Dom

António Brandão[27] in the mid-17th century from what had formerly been the farm-villa of the chief of Panelim's Hindu community and had been given by the Hindus to the clergy. Even in a ruined state, the façade seems to have been profusely decorated. The alternating windows and pilasters along the façade contrasts greatly with the dry austerity of the Archbishops' Palace in Goa.

The Abbot Cottineau de Kloguen, who stayed here at the invitation of Archbishop S. Galdino described the country palace this way: «*in front, the building has an excellent staircase, but inside there is only one floor in the form of a square cloister; the decorations are very beautiful, especially in the largest room, where the archbishop receives visitors.*»[28]

Despite the fact that there are so few examples, this Italianate aesthetic model, like the «chã» model before it, is an essential reference for understanding the evolution of Indo-

Above and left. *Alongside the great private chapel, this house presents a noteworthy veranda with solomonic columns showing strong ecclesiastical influence. Casa dos Machados, Nagoa*

[26] Apart from the photograph taken by Paul and De Sousa, there also exists a map showing the palace's location in the 1774 survey of the city of Goa, in the G. E. A. E. M.

[27] **Saldanha**, Padre M. J. Gabriel de, *História de Goa*, vol. II, *História Arqueológica*, New Goa, 1926, p. 13.

[28] **Kloguen**, Rev. Denis Cottinau de, *op. cit.*, p. 106.

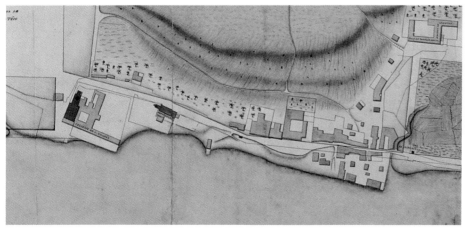

-Portuguese architecture. It is particularly important to the architecture that developed in the Bardez and Salcete provinces from the end of the 17th century until the 18th and 19th centuries, and which was the inspiration for most dwellings that exist today.

If plane architecture had its last phase of development during the period we call «restoration architecture» in Goa, the Mannerist style remained more operative in Goa. The new Academia da Fortificação (Academy of Fortifications), founded by King João IV seems to have had no echo in Goa. But the Jesuits and the architects they trained continued to be the propelling force behind of all fashionable architecture throughout the 18th century.

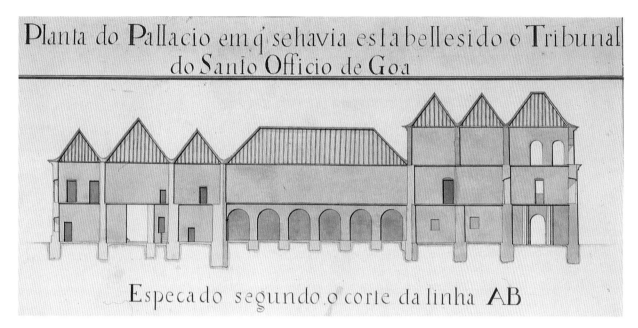

Planta do Pallacio em q̃ sehavia estabellesido o Tribunal do Santo Officio de Goa

Especado segundo o corte da linha AB

Left. Section of the Palácio da Inquisição, first residence of the Viceroys in Goa. Drawing from the second half of the 18ᵗʰ century. Gabinete de Estudos Históricos de Fortificação e Obras Militares

As its name indicates, this palace was the former residence of the Adil Shah (who was also known as Sabaio) in Goa. The viceroys used it as their residence before building the Palace of the Fortress. The Islamic structure seems to have been completely transformed; all the features that would have characterised it as Islamic having disappeared to such an extent that we find no sign of them either in palace inventories or in the oldest descriptions. Instead, the descriptions suggest a classical and Mannerist design with a tripartite façade and three main front doors, the largest being in the center. Analysing 18ᵗʰ century floor plans, it appears that the stone façade was not part of the original, early 16ᵗʰ century edifice. Renovated during a period more inclined towards Mannerism, the palace took on a refined, magnificent character when it passed from the viceroys into the hands of the Church. It was this renovation, in keeping with the profusely decorative style of 17ᵗʰ century religious architecture, that made the building the legend it is today. The palace had been initially organised around a central square courtyard, which again suggests a more classical concept than that of the 16ᵗʰ century «chã» palaces.

All the buildings inside the courtyard were progressively transformed into prisoners' cells.

Pyrard described the structure as follows: *«The Palace of the Inquisition is a very large building, with a beautiful main room; there is no king's house which has such a beautiful room.»*[29] It is regrettable that Pyrard gave no explanation for such praise, which once again reveals an ecclesiastic taste for great formal and decorative grandeur.

---

[29] **Pyrard de Laval**, *op. cit.*, p. 82.

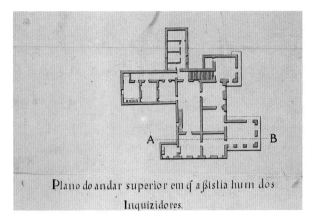

Plano do andar superior em q́ aßistia hum dos Inquizidores.

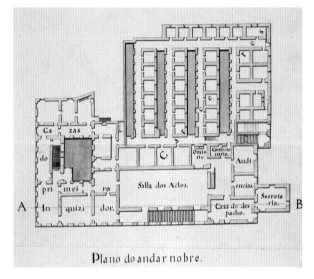

Plano do andar nobre.

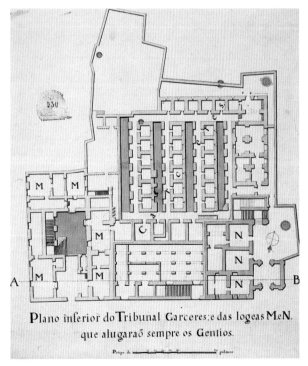

Plano inferior do Tribunal Carceres: e das logeas M e N. que alugaraõ sempre os Gentios.

Right. Plans of the Palácio da Inquisição from the second half of the 18ᵗʰ century. Gabinete de Estudos Históricos de Fortificação e Obras Militares

Tavernier, who had an audience with the Inquisitor, also described the interior of the palace: «*A page came to lead me to the great room, where after I walked around for about a quarter of an hour, an officer came to take me to the room where the Inquisitor was. After passing two galleries and several apartments, I entered a small room where the Inquisitor awaited me seated on the end of a large table in the shape of a billiard table, and both the table and all the other furniture in the room were covered with green cloth that is imported from England.*»[30]

Dellon, who was imprisoned in the palace, also left us a long description: «*The House of the Inquisition, which the Portuguese call Santa Casa, that is Holy House, is situated on one side of the town square in front of the cathedral dedicated to Saint Catherine. The house is large and magnificent; its façade has three doors, that of the middle being larger than the two others and the one by which one reaches the great stairway that leads to the great hall. The side doors lead to the inquisitors' apartments, each one being large enough to station a reasonably-sized train. Apart from these, there are other apartments for the officers of the house. Going further into the house, one finds a large building divided into several parts on two floors, each separated from the others by courtyards. On each floor there is a gallery in the form of a dormitory, divided into seven or eight small bedrooms, each one ten feet square, and there must be about 200 of these rooms.*»[31]

Like most of the palaces and grand buildings which resisted the decline of the 17ᵗʰ and 18ᵗʰ centuries, the inquisitors' palace was demolished in the 19ᵗʰ century because its size made its restoration too great a job for the modest colony that Goa had become.

---

[30] **Tavernier**, *op. cit.*, p. 141.
[31] Transcribed by **Fonseca**, José Nicolau da, *Sketch of the City of Goa*, New Delhi, 1986, p. 209.

This palace was the first country residence of the viceroys of Goa. Its location, facing inland and away from the Mandovi and from the sea, met the need for protection which lasted until the 17th century, when the palaces and leisure-time *quintas* began to be built closer to the banks.

Here we see an evolution comparable to that in Lisbon: the palaces of Queen Leonor and King João III in Xabregas are further inland, while the *quintas* built in Lisbon during the 17th and 18th centuries are found closer to the mouth of the Tagus River, between Santos and Belém.

Although only a few details are known about the Daugim palace, all indicate that this palace-residence on the banks of the Mandovi was designed in the Mannerist style. Lopes Mendes' engraving shows it, even though it was already in ruins, with molded pilasters and pediments above all the balcony windows on the first floor. Paintings in the Alpoim Galvão collection show the first floor resting on a classical arcade similar to that of the Goa customs house described by Pyrard, which he compares to the Place des Vosges in Paris.

The palace is also present, though only in a schematic form, in the map of Goa drawn by Linschoten at the end of the 16th century. These illustrations allow us to imagine an archway leading to the interior courtyard, as in the Palace of the Viceroy. It appears that the building was enlarged at the end of the 16th century, with this archway being placed in the center of the façade.

Left. *View of the Paço de Daugim, country estate of the Viceroys during the second half of the 16th century and the 17th century*

THE TRADITIONAL HINDU IV HOUSE MODEL

AND THE PREVAILING NATURE OF INDIGENOUS VALUES IN INDO-PORTUGUESE HOUSES

Contrary to their experiences in Africa and Brazil, the Portuguese were confronted in Goa by an ancient culture with a very hierarchical social structure and customs defined by particularly strict rules.

If the conversion to Catholicism provoked new behaviour on the part of the local population, the retention of the caste system maintained a number of social codes, particularly concerning domestic life. Even in the oldest examples of Indo-Portuguese houses built by Brahmin and Chardo families, the interior spatial layout conserves characteristics specific to local domestic architecture.

Behind a Portuguese-inspired façade, the interiors of these houses almost always reveal the expression of traditional Hindu customs, which still remain in the 20th century.

Indo-Portuguese civil architecture, the fruit of the cohabitation and inter-mingling of two civilisations, is in fact composed of two architectural models: a first, colonial and Portuguese, which we have already presented; and another, indigenous model.

In the context of reciprocal exchanges, the Portuguese culture affirms itself more forcefully in the façades of buildings, while the Hindu model influences the interiors, where one can see obvious and tenacious resistance to Portuguese spatial concepts.

The cultural confrontation gave birth to three distinct architectural types: the dwellings of converted Indian populations, the residences of Portuguese colonists, and finally the

Previous page. *Detail of the central patio* – raj angan – *in a Hindu house in Margão. Photo H. C.*
Above. *Small window of a Hindu house showing balusters of Portuguese influence. Photo, H. C.*

houses of Hindus who remained unconverted to Catholicism. If the last two are less numerous, they are nonetheless fundamental for understanding what we call the Indo-Portuguese house.

The Hindu house was traditionally constructed around an interior courtyard supported by columns, the *raj angan*. The building only presented the smallest windows and an entry door to the exterior. Even today, in the areas farthest from the «new conquests»[32], where the Portuguese influence was weaker and only showed itself during the second half of the 18th century, we find this type of house. Lopes Mendes, who visited these provinces at length in the mid-19th century, wrote: «*The houses are illuminated only by their doors and by the small, grilled windows in the largest of houses.*»[33]

Today, one can still find this type of house in the Hindu neighbourhoods of Mapuça and Margão. Even though the exteriors conform to Portuguese façade plans, the interiors are endowed with attributes typical of the Hindu traditional house. Domestic life in these houses is organised around the *raj angan*[34] in an open-air area surrounded by a colonnaded gallery called the *chouki*. Into this space open one or more wings with bedrooms, the *koudi*. Intimately linked to this patio is the *vasary*, the traditional dining room, linked in turn to the temple or the dressed altar in the heart of the house. The ritual nature of the place explains why the altar is often found in the back of this room. We find the same configuration later in

Above. All the decorative detailing of the pilasters, columns, frames and capitals bear witness to a profound internfluence between Hindu and Christian styles. Shanta Durga Temple in Queulá. Photo Paul and De Sousa Archives, Pangim

[32] *Nouvelles conquêtes*, see p. 107.

[33] **Mendes**, A. Lopes, *op. cit.*, vol. II, p. 136.

[34] This term, used to designate the open-air patio, varies according to different authors. **Bragança Pereira**, in *Etnografia da Índia Portuguesa*, vol. II, p. 81, uses the term of *razan gonn*, perhaps from konkâni nomenclature. The term *raj angan* is, however, the term most commonly used by Hindu families.

Catholic Brahmin houses such as those of the Miranda family in Loutulim and the Cabrais family in Nagoa.

Situated in the interior of the house, the *vasary* also communicates with the kitchen. This space has huge importance in Hindu culture because of the caste system and the ban on «impure» contacts. The ritual of meals in the Hindu tradition, and above all in the Brahmin caste, has always taken place in a specific part of the house, whose proportions and rules are strictly defined.

These rules, linked to the purity of blood, had particular importance because they were not simply of a moral order. One error in this domain, as absurd as it might seem to Western eyes, could entail the excommunication of a family member by the *Suamy*, the religious dignitary. The excommunicated member would be considered dead for the rest of the community, stripped of his rights and property, and disgrace would befall the entire family.

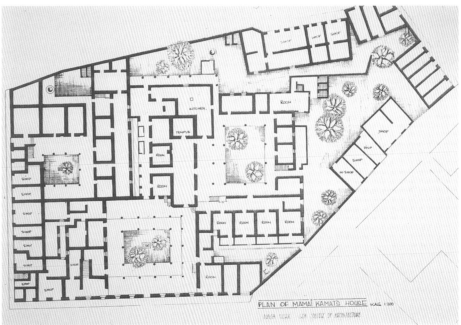

Above. *Of Oriental style, the columns of the main patio denote a plane architectural influence from the 17th century. Central patio and plan of the Palácio dos Mamai Kamat in Pangim. Survey carried out by the students of the Pangim Faculty of Architecture*

IV-1 THE «VASARY», A PERMANENT ELEMENT IN INDO-PORTUGUESE CIVIL ARCHITECTURE

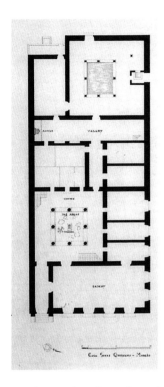

The maintenance of the caste system by Christianised Indians explains why the *vasary* kept its importance and its value as a fundamental element of interior spaces. The fact that in European culture the dining room only became an entity at the end of the 18th century helped families to retain the *vasary* in the Indo-Portuguese house, making its role, placement and shape indelible.

This long room, three times as long as it was wide, owes its form to the ritual of the meals which were served in a long line.[35] Even today, the translation of the Portuguese expression to sit down for a meal corresponds in Concanim as «eating in line.» While Hindu domestic architectural models evolved or changed in the houses built by Brahmins and Chardos during the 18th and 19th centuries, the *vasary* remained

unchanged and became a specific element of Indo-Portuguese architecture.

Houses of the largest size also contained a *sadery*, a reception room, normally reserved for such events as marriages and christenings. The profoundly private nature of Hindu domestic life placed this room apart from the other rooms. It was usually located on the first floor, separated from the domestic living areas, near the guest rooms. Such placement permitted the family to limit its contacts with outsiders.[36]

---

[35] **Feio**, Mariano, *As Castas Hindus de Goa*, Lisbon, 1979, p. 37.
[36] *Ibid*, p. 38.

Above. Plan of a traditional Hindu house in Margão. Survey, At. H. C.
Right. Central patio of a Hindu house in Margão covered in screens on the first floor level. Photo H. C.

Following page. View of the Palácio dos Rane in Sanquelim with, in the foreground, a small turret of obvious Portuguese influence

Above and right. *Two details of the architectural complex of the Palácio dos Rane in Sanquelim. Photo H. C.*

This traditional model can be perfectly seen in the houses of Goa's old families who were never converted to Christianity, such as the Mamal Kamat or the Dempó families.

It is interesting in the framework of our study to analyse the houses of Brahmin families who resisted the pressure of the Catholic church. While we can recognise in it an internal structure belonging to the purest Hindu tradition, the façade does belie Portuguese influence. This resemblance in the façade, with the adoption of windows and pilasters of Mannerist inspiration, is found in Hindu family houses outside former Portuguese territories. The palace of the Rane de Sanquelim is an example of this mixture of styles, and that even in a family that for centuries fought the Portuguese presence in India. The Rane came originally from Rajahstan, the descendants of rajahs and members of the *kshatriya* warrior caste. The Rane de Sanquelim palace is naturally composed of elements from the

Rajahstan region, where the Moghul influence was strong. That explains the small arched windows in the oldest part of the house. Belonging to a family of warrior chiefs, and composed of several independent buildings, this dwelling more closely resembles a fortress than a palace.

Portuguese influences appear nonetheless, however, in one part of the palace where the balcony windows alternate with pilasters – language clearly inspired by the Mannerist palaces of Goa. In another part of the palace reserved for women is a watchtower where the Portuguese influence is equally obvious.

In the houses of families such as the Dessay de Arabó, Lamargão or Collem, who also fought the Portuguese, the same influences prevail. They bear witness to the numerous peacetime periods which, throughout the centuries, allowed the colonisers to propagate their culture beyond the territories they administered.

In certain Goa interiors belonging to Hindus, even though rigorously maintained with strict traditions, Portuguese influence is still apparent. In the *raj angan* of the Mamal Kamat palace, the columns have Portuguese-inspired lines and proportions. In entering the courtyard, a visitor immediately has the impression of being transported to a farm in the Alentejo, because of the size of the white-washed columns, with their bases and capitals

painted in ochre, and because of the overall design of the court.

But in these Hindu houses outside the Portuguese-controlled zone, it is the façades – their composition, design and hierarchy of volumes – that the Lusitanian influence shows itself most clearly. Interior spaces resisted the foreign influence, even in those houses owned by Indians who had converted to the Portuguese faith and customs. This double sentiment of acceptance and rejection gave birth to a metamorphising process with an architecture which appeared to be Portuguese but which, on the inside, remained profoundly Indian.

Above. *Detail of the temple integrated in the Palácio dos Rane in Sanquelim. Photo H. C.*

INDO-PORTUGUESE CIVIL ARCHITECTURE V

AND THE FORMATION OF PERMANENT FEATURES

The «chã» and Mannerist aesthetics, which inspired Portuguese civil architecture in the Indies during the 16th and 17th centuries, both underwent profound modifications in the political, cultural and economic climate that differed so radically from Europe.

From this interaction was born an architecture which adapted itself over time while still retaining the characteristics of each of its ancestors in a complex family of influences. In the «chã» model we have seen that the Portuguese in India gradually adopted social behaviour aimed at rivaling, both in pomp and etiquette, that of India's high castes. This competition created a flexibility which adapted itself to the entire cultural context, architecture included. And it was this ability to adapt which allowed European aesthetic models to transform, integrating as they did some of the characteristics and aesthetic values of the Hindu and Islamic models.

The *vasary*, that interior space of utmost importance to the Indian household, was now introduced in the spatial layout of Portuguese architecture, where Portuguese builders interpreted it as a covered veranda. This opening of the house onto its gardens is present in the Palácio do Deão (dean's palace), and in the floor plan of the Powder House palace.

The placement of a chapel in Portuguese houses here also reveals a strong Indian influence: the altar to the ancestors occupied a primordial place in the Hindu interior space, because it was used daily in various domestic ceremonies.

Left. *Veranda covered with screens. Casa dos Proença in Calangute*

Above. Forming part of a vast set of 16ᵗʰ and 17ᵗʰ century buildings which have disappeared, this photograph of the Catcúmenes School in Betim are witness to the typical character of the folded roofs in all Indo-Portuguese architecture until the 19ᵗʰ century. Paul and De Sousa Archives, Pangim

In the houses of colonists of noble rank, the chapel progressively acquired an intimacy and rapport with the rest of the interior space, unlike those in any houses in Europe. This relationship developed in Indo-Portuguese houses during the 18ᵗʰ century, as the chapel became integrated in the sequence of sitting rooms, and eventually opened directly onto them.

In the dean's palace, as in certain Brahmin houses, the chapel occupies the central location, immediately beyond the front entrance.

India's hot, humid climate also had its role in transforming Portuguese building habits. Taking on some Indian house features was almost a necessity for coping with the unaccustomed heat.

The Italian sculptor Ramponi, who came to Goa accompanying the tomb of Saint Francis Xavier offered by the Grand Duke of Tuscany, gave in his journal a vision of civil architecture here. Speaking of Goa in 1698, he wrote: *«The houses were built with only two floors, their walls being made of dried earth and mortar and the blocks placed one upon the other; on the exterior they are covered and whitened with a mixture made of oyster shells, producing a sort of lime, as white as the snow, so white, in truth, that if one walks through the city during the hours of bright sunlight , the whiteness hurts one's eyes... The servants and the black slaves live on the ground floor, of beaten earth, and their masters live on the floor above... the roofs are pointed and the red brick tiles are placed like fish scales, which is not at all unpleasant to see...»*[37]

Continuing his description, Ramponi indicated clearly that the buildings had high roofs, pointed and steeply inclined, as well as large galleries, verandas and porches, which together provided ventilation and cooling for the interior.

[37] **Ramponi**, Plácido Francesco, «Um Artista Italiano em Goa» in *Garcia de Orta*, Lisbon, 1956, pp. 300-301.

Della Valle, describing Goan architecture, said that «*the buildings are good, large and adequate, built for the most part to welcome the breeze and fresh air, which is absolutely necessary given the great heat and also the great rains during monsoon season...*»[38]

This explicit evocation of an architecture conceived to take in breezes and fresh air refers to the sweeping verandas and galleries that opened on to the gardens and rear courts of the houses.

In contrast to the arid façades, the rest of the buildings often opened onto gardens and courtyards *(patios)* to adapt to the region's climactic conditions. Gemelli Carreri[39] spoke of the archbishops' country palace in Panelim, describing the magnificence of the salons and the numerous galleries from which one could admire the banks of the Mandovi River. The

galleries appear clearly in a photograph of the palace dating from the 19th century and published in 1933 in a book on the archdiocese of Goa. The gallery, composed of an arrangement of imposing pillars, was entirely enclosed by large sash windows. The gallery-veranda of the palace of the Counts of Nova Goa is another interesting example, even though we only know it through old pictures and documents. The palace is described in Lopes Mendes' book and appears in a photograph of Paul and De Sousa. The veranda opened onto a garden running the length of the façade, and was entirely covered by wooden screens inlaid with *carepas* (the mother-of-pearl linings of oyster shells and other shells, finely polished). Pyrard also highlighted these galleries in his writings,

Above. The alternation of pilasters with windows crowned still by triangulat pediments which are only found in Portugal in particularly academic buildings, appears here as a systematic feature of Indo-Portuguese architecture. The Palácio dos Cárcome Lobo, now disappeared, in a drawing by Lopes Mendes in his book Índia Portuguesa.
Left. *Detail of a typical structure of a wall in laterite. Colva Church. Photo H. C.*

---

[38] **Valle**, *op. cit.*, p. 155.
[39] **Carreri**, Gemelli, *Giro delle Mondo*, Venice, 1719. Vol. III, p. 63.

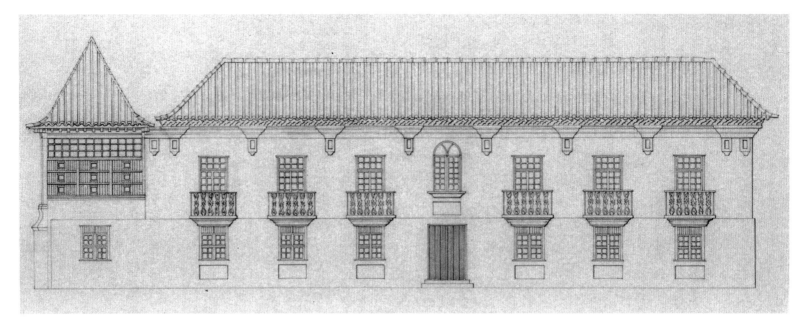

saying: «*The most common pastime for women is to spend all day at the windows, which they call ventanas, which are exceedingly lovely, large and spacious, in the form of galleries or balconies, with shutters and screens painted very prettily, so that the women can see without being seen.*»[40]

In the house of the Proença family in Calangute, in the province of Bardez, one can also observe a veranda in the shape of a tower, entirely covered in *carepas*. In the Santana da Silva palace at Margão, the veranda runs the length of the lateral façade, but the screens of *carepas* have been replaced by glass.

These galleries and semi-open spaces were considered by the Portuguese to be indispensable to their health and well-being. The royal hospital, which numerous visitors during Goa's golden era at the end of the 16th and the beginning of the 17th centuries described as a luxurious palace where patients ate from China plates, also had vast galleries open to permit air to circulate.

Without the accounts of travelers and a handful of illustrations, the Doyen palace would remain the most significant example of these structures. This edifice, built during the second half of the 18th century by a rich Portuguese prelate from Braga, has a complex assembly of galleries, parlors and colonnaded verandas which allow us to imagine the other palaces built in the same period with greater financial means.

The steeply sloped roofs of these ample galleries had the function of aerating the house interiors. These roofs, which took the name «scissor» *(tesoura)* in Portuguese, are an interesting element of Indo-Portuguese archi-

Above and right. Elevation and plan of the Casa dos Proença in Calangute. Survey by At. H. C.

[40] **Pyrard de Laval**, *op. cit.*, p. 187.

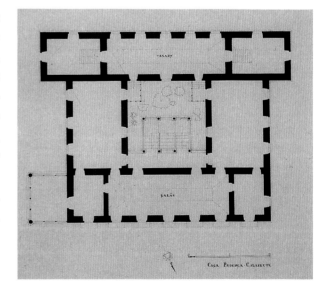

tecture, which would be exported to other corners of the empire and would even influence architecture back home in Portugal.

Crowned by very high, pyramidal ceilings, the rooms benefitted from the continual breezes which entered through the windows and rose towards the ceiling. The method of placing roof tiles in scale patterns permitted hot air to escape.

In the 19th century, scissor roofs were slowly replaced by less inclined roofs. The principal reason for their replacement was the fact that they were so difficult and dangerous to maintain. Even though it no longer has its seven original roofs, the Santana da Silva palace is today one of the last examples of this roofing style that was once so common among palaces and convents.

In the 19th century drawings collected in the work *Índia portuguesa* and in the photographs in Paul and De Sousa's albums of the end of the century, we can see this peaked roof on most of the old buildings; it was therefore in current building use until the end of the 18th century. The paintings in the Alpoim Galvão collection, dating from the early 19th century, show the systematic presence of these roofs on the large palaces along the Mandovi.

Above and left. *Detail of a veranda coverd by screens and drawing of the Casa dos Proença in Calangute. Author's drawing*

During the 19th century, the method seemed to change. Builders started to use a straighter type of tile called *mangalor*, and ventilators were installed on the new roofs, a procedure still used on houses today. Modifications linked to the ventilation systems were also made to the balcony windows. Shutters were devised that allowed inhabitants to open only the bottom half to circulate the air and increase the temperature difference between the air which entered and that which accumulated in the highest part of the ceiling.

As for construction material, Goa was not endowed with good quality stone. This lack was compensated by using a light, porous stone called laterite; easy to cut and therefore easy to use. Traditional masonry of adobe or cement using stone was reserved to less important dwellings. While Ramponi reported that the buildings were in adobe, other foreigners explained with more precision that the important buildings were built in laterite, as did Biervillas: *«All the churches, hospitals, colleges, and public buildings, as well as the houses of the Portuguese and Creoles, are built of a bastard type of reddish marble, mixed with cut stones.»*[41]

The structural and decorative value of a house's external corners, which in Portuguese architecture from the 16th to 18th centuries had definite significance, melted little by little into an entirely stone structure, and the same thing happened to the façade. The substitution of corners on the ends of the façade for a double pilaster as well as the application of Mannerist-derived pilasters all along the façade owe their popularity to the technical possibilities offered by laterite. The rising taste for decorative exuberance and the availability of qualified

[41] **Biervillas**, Innigo de, *Voyage à la Côte du Malabar*, Paris, 1736.

labour at reasonable prices allowed the development of the most extravagant ornamental effects, for which Indian artisans were particularly talented.

The double pilaster on each end of a house's façade, as well as the alternating window-pilaster effect, were progressively enhanced with molding, fluting and capitals up until the Baroque and even the Romantic epochs.

Laterite's porosity was compensated for with the use of a type of lime made of oyster shells very resistant to the rains and the humidity of the monsoons. Even today, after monsoon season, all the churches and large houses are systematically repainted. This lime made a stucco that was strong and resistant to rain. The technical possibilities of laterite and stucco permitted the development of a new, ornamentally profuse language which became a specialty of religious and civil architecture.

In addition to this new, highly Indian decoration, civil architecture here took on other elements that distinguished it from that in Portugal, and that make it uniquely Indo-Portuguese.

Verandas and screened windows, mentioned by writers as early as the 17th century, compensated for the lack of glass. They bear witness to the great creativity of Portuguese architecture, as well as to its capacity to adapt to the most varied geographic and cultural conditions.

The windows built from a wooden grill filled with small bits of oyster shell placed in a fish-scale pattern gave a pleasing light and still permitted the vital circulation of air in this hot, humid climate.

Like the folded roofs, the screens suggested, by their shape and structure, Islamic origins. When the first Portuguese conquered Goa, the city was a large commercial centre serving the entire Malabar coast. But it is surprising that travelers who described India between the 16th and 18th centuries only spoke of *carepas* when describing Portuguese cities. In Surate, which had been Muslim like Goa, these *carepas* don't seem to have been used. Jean Henri Grose affirmed that in Surate, *«they have European-style mirrors, of which they are very proud.»*[42]

But we must not forget that the Portuguese still had, during the 16th century, carpentry traditions of Moorish influence. Many of the

___
[42] **Grose**, Jean Henri, *Voyages aux Indes Orientales*, 1753.

Above. *Design of a façade based on a mannerist double pilaster style introduced into India through religious architecture. Casa dos Gama Pinto in Saligão. Photo H. C.*

Previous page. *Central nucleus of entrance and stairs in central patio. Casa dos Proença in Calangute*

first fortresses erected on the Malabar coast were in wood and made in Portugal. Afonso de Albuquerque, in a letter to Dom Manuel, asked him to send *«a wooden castle that can house fifty to sixty men.»*[43] These constructions, of which we know of several examples, demanded sophisticated woodwork and carpentry techniques so that they could be transported in the hulls of ships and assembled on arrival.

The system of roof beams in the ceiling, derived from the Islamic tradition of *«de laços»* or fan tracery ceilings, common in Portugal in the 16th century, can also be found in Goa. Rather than being composed of a series of horizontal beams, these roofs are held up by four beams joining the walls in the corners of a room. The ceilings thereby became more ample, crowned by a pyramidal form more adapted to the Indian climate.

The restraining beams of these roofs were sculpted following Hindu aesthetic traditions, but punctuated by the most remarkable angels' heads and other symbols of Christian iconography.

The abundance of hard and resistant woods, much used because of the lack of iron, favored the use of wooden balustrades for balconies. Mannerist-style iron balustrades were copied and painted, and the resulting curiosities were described by voyagers. We find them also in palaces such as those of the kings of Sundém and in various sites in Ribandar.

As for the structures and the foundations of these buildings, here we can also note an adaptation to the local resources and techniques. As in Indian architecture, the buildings were erected on a large socle made of blocks which were solid protection against the infiltration of water and the invasion of growing plants.

The near-disappearance of civil Indo-Portuguese architecture makes it difficult to build rigorous definitions concerning their structures. We must therefore content ourselves with characterisations of the architecture by drawing upon its architectonic and ornamental elements. Analysis of all the documentation of the period indicates, however, the existence of two distinct models: one clearly inspired by the

[43] *As Gavetas da Torre de Tombo,* I, Lisbon, 1965, p. 302.

Portuguese model of a noble house, which we will call *casa de sobrado* (two-storey house), and another in which is present the traditional Hindu mode of dwelling, the *casa de patio* (house with courtyard), with a single, ground floor.

Above. *Interior of a veranda covered by screens. Casa dos Proença, Calangute.*
Photo H. C.

V-1 THE ART OF LIVING
AND DECORATIVE ARTS

Above. *Aspect of slatted features to allow circulation of air. Casa dos Costas in Parra. Photo H. C.*
Right. *17th century Indo-Portuguese chair. Monteiros de Candolim private collection. Photo H. C.*

With most of Goa's 16th and 17th century palaces having disappeared, it is relatively difficult to accurately describe their interior characteristics. The interdependence of religious and civil architecture suggests, however, that the Church's pomp and its taste for magnificence might have an influence on the grand houses of the Portuguese nobility.

The availability of cheap manual labour in Goa, and the development of a group of artisans, particularly in cabinetry, allowed the colonists easy recourse to decorative arts. In this port city where all Portuguese trade with the Orient was centred, access to the most precious textiles and objects such as Chinese porcelains enriched local creativity even more.

The ostentation of the aristocracy showed itself primarily in public life, however, because domestic daily life until the 17th century was strictly private and protected from any contact with strangers. Such was even more rigidly the case for women. As in Portugal, ladies of the highest rank left their houses only exceptionally, and always accompanied by a large escort, or under the cover of a litter.

Grand houses only opened themselves to strangers for exceptional events, and even in those cases the women were rarely presented to the guests. This custom explains why foreign visitors to Goa left so little in the way of descriptions of the interiors of houses or palaces.

The references to the Palace of the Viceroys only concern the two rooms open to visitors: the audience hall with its portraits of governors, and the antechamber with the paintings

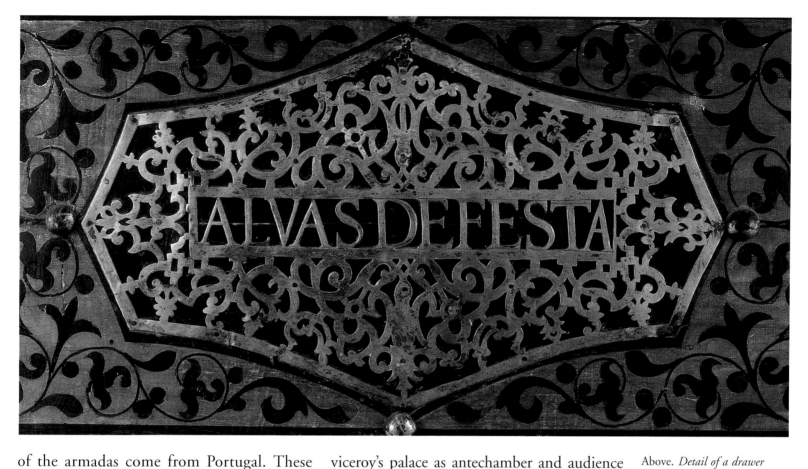

of the armadas come from Portugal. These paintings were, as Diogo do Couto explained in one of his letters, purely decorative, because when they were in very bad condition they were restored in less than a month. This type of painting was common in private buildings and in churches; Indian families in Goa would keep up the tradition until the 18th and 19th centuries. The current Palace of the Archbishops has the remains of frescoes and a plaster decoration imitating fabric.

A rare case among the foreigners visiting Goa, Mandeslslo was received by the viceroy and then invited to dinner at the house of a member of the high nobility. He described how, after dinner, the guests moved into *«a large room, where he invited (them) to drink...»*[44] The room where supper was served and the parlor to which they retired afterwards were the large reception rooms, designed along the same models as those cited so often in the viceroy's palace as antechamber and audience hall. They constituted the house's public area; the long veranda-room turned towards the gardens being the private area, the place of daily life, where the women of the house lived surrounded by their children and their slaves.

Mandelslo also remembered of the dinner party that *«the palaces of the nobles are truly magnificent, but particularly in their furniture.»*[45] The reference to the quality of the furnishings is partly due to the gifts offered by the Portuguese noble to the chief of the delegation of which Mandelslo was a member: *«a beautiful table and a handsome lacquer cabinet.»*[46]

Unlike palace interiors, descriptions of the royal hospital, a public building, are numerous. Accounts detailing its interior, but also its

Above. *Detail of a drawer from a large chest. Sacristy of the Bom Jesus de Goa Church*

---

[44] **Mandelslo**, *Voyage des Indes du Sr. de....*, book II, p. 255.
[45] *Ibid.* p. 263.
[46] *Ibid.* p. 255.

services, furniture, and the variety and quality of the bedsheets and patients' robes, as well as the Chinese porcelain table services, gave the impression of great civility. Pyrard, who stayed there as a patient, affirmed: «*This hospital is the most beautiful, I think, in the world, be it for the grace of the building and its dependencies, all well organised, or for the rule of order there, the cleanliness, the great care taken of the sick, the help or consolation for everything one could desire, be it the medicine, drugs and remedies for recovering one's health and the meat sold there, or for the spiritual consolation one may have in timely fashion.*»[47]

Vincent Le Blanc, who claimed to have traveled around the world for decades, added that even «*that of the Holy Spirit in Rome, nor the infirmary of Malta, where one is served on silver dishes, can be equal to this one in richness, order and service.*»[48]

The unanimity of opinion on the Royal Hospital allows us to imagine the care of the organisation and daily use of furniture without equal in Europe. When Pyrard was there, the hospital housed nearly 1,500 patients. In the rooms, «*the beds are covered in lacquer and red varnish, some are brightly colored, some are gilded; the straps supporting the mattresses are made of cotton, and the pillows filled with cotton, the mattresses and blankets of silk or cotton canvas, decorated with all sorts of figures and colors... All the beds are in one big place, with their straps rolled up; in another are the pillows, in another the mattresses, blankets and shrouds, shirts and other linens for hospital use.*»[49]

If the author doesn't precisely describe the pieces of furniture, he says that they were of the same type as those used in grand houses, and worthy of praise. This type of furniture, known later as Indo-Portuguese, was exported in great quantities to Portugal and was of greater quality than much furniture in European production.

The chaise, which in the Portugal of the 16th and 17th centuries kept its hierarchic character – those with arms and backs being reserved for the high aristocracy – became more democratic in Goa.

Along with furniture, textiles seem to have had pride of place in Goan houses, which does not come as a surprise; during the same period, the Portuguese at home covered their parlors with silk, always in strong colors, and sometimes even painted.

[47] **Pyrard de Laval**, *op. cit.*, p. 7.

[48] **Le Blanc**, Vincent, *Les Voyages Fameux du Sr...* Paris, 1648, p. 75.

[49] **Pyrard de Laval**, *op. cit.*, p. 5 and pp. 14-15.

Civil architecture of the 17th century was characterised by the apparition of two models of noble houses, whose forms would be definitive by the 18th century. Influenced by «chã» forms and Mannerist taste, the new models also incorporated Hindu spatial values. The Hindu house form was the real foundation for the *casa de pátio* with, naturally, a few values of «chã» and Mannerist architecture incorporated.

The first model that we will call *casa de sobrado* is essentially the Portuguese nobles' house, with two storeys. The ground floor was generally for services and servants, while the first floor was for the lord of the house. Ram-

poni referred to this style in his description of noble houses in Goa, as we have seen.[50]

This hierarchy is reinforced on the main façade with a decorative ranking of the upper floor with windows opening onto balconies, while on the ground floor the windows are not floor length, they start at waist-height, and are decorated or framed very simply.

In Portugal until the 17th century, and in Brazil until the 19th, the mere designation *sobrado* signified «noble house». Such was not the case in India, where another form of noble

---

[50] **Ramponi**, *op. cit.*, pp. 300-301.

Above and left. *Both the dentils of the cornice from the façade as well as the grooves in the pilasters are clearly different from Portuguese civil architecture. Casa dos Pintos in Santa Cruz.
Photo H. C.*

square courtyard, as Kloguen underlined in his description.[52] The fact that the house had originally been the farm of a rich Brahmin explains the strong Hindu influence on it.

This form differs strongly from the other noble house model that developed around a court and whose main façade is less effectively highlighted.

The first floor differs radically in these two models. While in the *casa de sobrado* the upper floor is a fundamental and characteristic element, the *casa de pátio* is systematically composed of one sole storey; a rare configuration in the Portuguese noble house.

Intimately linked to a symbolism of power, the *casa de sobrado* was always the preferred form for the large urban palaces of the nobility, while their country estates, where the image of power was less a requirement, often took the *casa de pátio* configuration.

The *casa de sobrado* seems therefore to have adopted a stricter, more sober «chã» aesthetic, closer to Portuguese norms, while Mannerist tendencies developed more freely in the country *quintas*.

Among the rare examples of construction prior to the 18th century, the house of the Monteiro de Candolim family is a precious cases of 17th century building where the *casa de pátio* style manifests itself in all its force. The fact that the Monteiros de Candolim family was a Christian Brahmin family demonstrates again the Hindu origin of this type of house.

By comparing this Indian-owned example with old images and with details of houses since altered, it is possible to identify the norms of country houses built by Portuguese

house existed on one floor only, arranged around a courtyard: the *casa de pátio*.

It is interesting to compare the façade design of the Cárcome Lobo palace with that of the *quinta* that the same family owned in Dandim.[51] While the palace has a long, two-storey body in «chã» style, the farm is a low, one-storey grouping around a central court. One sees the same difference in city and country styles between the archbishops' palace in Goa and their estate in Panelim, which was originally a farmhouse. The Panelim residence was two-storeys high, but its rooms were all on the upper floor, distributed around a central,

[51] **Mendes**, A. Lopes, *A Índia Portuguesa*, Lisbon, 1886. The palace in São Pedro is shown in vol. I, p. 174. The Dandim quinta is in vol. II, shown from two angles, on p. 164 and p. 166.

[52] **Kloguen**, Rev. Denis Cottineau de, *op. cit.*, p. 107.

families in the same period. The Portuguese house norms were the dominant aesthetic during the 17th century, even though they themselves were influenced by Hindu architecture. Located outside of the area on which Goa had direct influence, where the most erudite and luxurious examples were found, this house was linked to the powerful Pinto family, close cousins of the Monteiros. It was among these families, grouped around the Pintos, that indigenous values began to assert themselves.

The particularly elaborate design of the façade of this house, reflecting the classicism of its interior structure, is the most erudite example of Mannerist influence in Portuguese India.

The windows surmounted by pediments, with busts in their tympani, the fluted pilasters and Corinthian capitals, the alternating rhythm of pilasters and windows – all reinforced by an overarching refinement of design – are very close to the Italian Mannerist spirit, and without an equivalent in Portugal. Like the façade design, the interior presents an original organisation, as the junction of two buildings. To a first and salient rectangular block, in European tradition, is added a second block turned towards the courtyard and developing out of the *vasary*, in keeping with Hindu tradition. The independence of each of these two bodies is a timid example of how these two profoundly different architectural models would develop over the course of the 18th and 19th centuries. The Monteiros house in Candolim is still the most refined and interesting example of the Indo-Portuguese house. Even though it is clearly of the 17th century,

the house presents the courtyard structure and a single-storey development characteristic of Hindu houses.

If throughout the 18th century the *casa de sobrado* model remained the reference point for building, the *casa de pátio* developed little by little to become, in the 19th century, the norm and archetype of the Indo-Portuguese house.

Above. *Detail of a window and pilasters emphasising a 17th century mannerist tradition, unparalleled in Portuguese civil architecture built in Portugal. Casa dos Monteiros in Candolim. Photo H. C.*

V-3   THE TOWER HOUSE
AS COLONIAL ARCHAISM

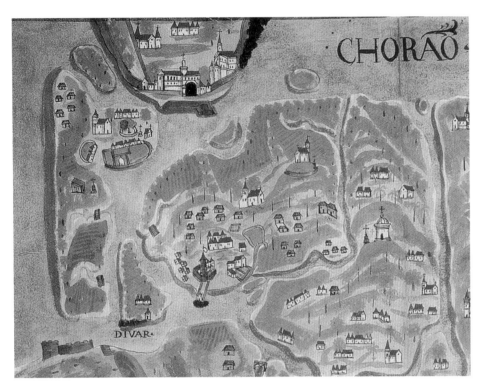

In addition to the architectural styles represented by the two-storey and patio houses, Goa spawned a third design, that of the tower-house. Limited to a very few examples, its distinctive features may still be observed. This ancient design had its local roots in the first public buildings of the 16ᵗʰ century, and as it evolved it also assumed features of the Hindu house. Its design nucleus and visual centerpiece was a fortified turret, intended for defense.

The focal point of the Casa dos Lobos in Anjuna is a tower with particularly thick walls, whose internal staircase leads to a windowless room with embrasures for firing harquebuses. The house's residential area leads off from the tower and, judging from its layout and its thinner walls, must have been later additions.

An 18ᵗʰ century survey of the palace-fortress of the Viceroys in Goa clearly shows the structure of two great towers, that century's improvement on the already-archaic concept of the tower-house.

Similarly, the drawings of fortresses and garrisons in Gaspar Correia's *Lendas da Índia*, though sketched in a more naturalistic style, depict houses belonging to captains or governors, some of which were endowed with one or more towers.

Lack of safety in the Bardez and Salcete provinces during the 16ᵗʰ and 17ᵗʰ centuries would have led captains from these provinces to house themselves in small towers rather than conventionally-designed residences. With such a tower-house in Goa, a captain had a place to spend the night during a tour of duty which, in an emergency, could house a detachment of troops. But a shortage of stone in the region caused the towers to lose their defensive functions, and the practice of building them all but vanished.

However, the tower-house appears to be the origin for a small group of houses which are utterly distinct from the region's more typical two-storey houses, which developed horizontally, and from the patio houses, which, as their name implies, radiate outward from an interior patio.

The remaining examples of the turreted house style are two-storey houses characterised by a large room on the upper storey which is independent from the rest of the house. In the oldest surviving example, the Lobos house in Anjuna, the large room is the only elevated room, while the rest of the house extends only along the ground floor.

In its later development, this large room was influenced by the *sadery* of the traditional Hindu house. Accessible directly from the entrance hall, the large room shed its defensive nature to take on the stately functions of parties and ceremonies. Its independence from the house's other rooms allowed it to receive guests of other castes while preserving the house's living quarters from the risk of breaking household rules on purity of blood.

Of this small group of houses, there is one interesting example in the province of Bardez: the Casa dos Sousa in Siolim. The engraved date of 1770 on the entrance balcony over the door confirms either the period of the house's construction, or of significant alterations to the building. The reception room, on two floors, is covered by a hipped-roof, using a system of wooden trusses placed closely together in the tradition of the region's folded roofs.

In the province of Salcete, near the Seminário de Rachol, there is another house of this type: the Casa dos Mascarenhas. The presence of a large chapel detached from the house, as well as some of its interior details, despite rebuilding during the last century, suggest that the house dates from the 17th century. The house's proximity to the convent at Rachol may be explained as a protective shelter for priests, but also makes the case for confirming the previous existence of a fortress.

Still another example is the Casa dos Silveiras, which confirms the practice, established in the previously mentioned houses, of a conformity of the interior plan from which a balconied entrance unfolds from and depends on the first floor reception room, while a group of living rooms are formed in the opposite direction, and the service infrastructure is relegated to the rear.

Below. *Plan and detail of the façade of the Casa dos Lobos in Anjuna. Survey by At. H. C.*

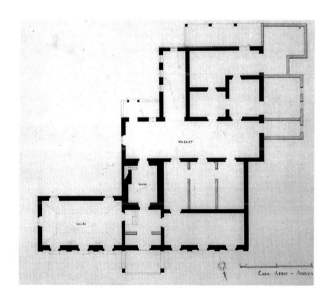

CASA MONTEIROS. CANDOLIM

Arranged around a courtyard with a chapel, the Monteiros family house presents 17th century characteristics of a very high aesthetic quality. The chapel dedicated to Nossa Senhora dos Agonizantes (Our Lady of the Dying) was opened for public worship by a papal bull of Pope Clement XI in 1714, which also confirmed the powers of this family at the time. The house and the chapel predate the bull; they were built in the period when the Monteiro family were linked to the Pinto family, the richest and most powerful family of the region. Pascoal Pinto, born in 1645, married Francisca Monteiro; it was doubtless as a result of this union that the house has the lustre that it still exudes today.

The erudite design of the Monteiro house is perhaps derived from the prestige the family enjoyed among the ranks of the high clergy,

but also from the lovely dwelling it owned in Candolim, of which only the chapel remains today. The revolt of 1794, also known as the revolt of the Pinto thanks to the participation of several Pinto family members, hastened the dwelling's ruin. It surely served as a model for the Monteiros house and that of the Frias family, also linked to the Pintos.

As for its structure, the edifice is composed of two nearly independent groupings inspired by profoundly different aesthetic concepts. The first, clearly of classical and Mannerist influence, houses the rooms that were used for social occasions and presenting the family's image to outsiders. It is composed of a rectangle with three façades, each with balconied windows alternating with pilasters. The second, with fewer openings toward the

Above and left. Detail of the façade and drawing of the Casa dos Monteiros in Candolim

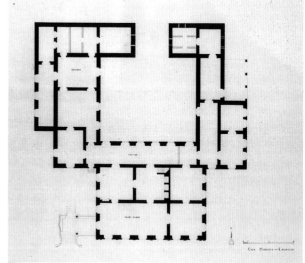

Above and right. Elevation, plan and view of Capela-casa dos Monteiros in Candolim. Survey by At. H. C.

exterior, is larger and focused towards the interior, along a courtyard whose spatial concepts are clearly derived from Hindu tradition. The traditional *vasary* links the two very different building groups.

Contrary to what we can see in older, 17th century houses, where Portuguese norms are predominant, the norms of the Hindu tradi-tion are more clearly manifest here, as though to affirm a pride of race that families linked to the Pintos always claimed.

In this house, we find the single-storey *casa de pátio* model, which would become the norm in the 19th century. This house type was more easily adapted to the Hindu way of life, which insists that the *vasary* be directly linked to the kitchen and its dependencies, separating hierarchically the two parts with several steps.

The balance and the aesthetic quality of the three façades and the house's other details make this building an important architectural specimen of Goa's 17th century *quintas* and country palaces, which are now for the most part vanished or heavily transformed. On the main floor, the windows on the balconies that are capped with well-proportioned triangular pediments are a perfect presentation for the series of relief busts in the purest classical tradition. While this pediment type is present in churches and some palaces, the Monteiro house busts are the only ones to survive for us. This must not, however, have been an exceptional case, because in the Santana da Silva palace there are busts on the imposts of the doors on the grand stairway.

Inside, the sitting room and public rooms use the Arabic tradition of *«de laços»* ceilings with sculpted beams, a technique we find in the Palace of the Archbishops in Goa and which lasted until the middle of the 18th century. In one of the entertaining rooms is found, in a niche, a private chapel in 17th century cut stone, which attests to the age of the house. By the 18th century, these oratories were normally built of gilded wood, without the rigor and severity of the previous century.

We can also see in this house a collection of 17th century Indo-Portuguese armchairs, as

Left. *Witnessing its antiquity, as with the academic aspect of the house, the reception room displays paintings on sgrafitto stucco work identical to those in the Palácio dos Arcebispos in Goa. Interior detail of the reception room's window, Casa dos Monteiros in Candolim. Photo H. C.*

well as a remarkable canopy bed with Hindu decoration composed of nail heads, where the gable ends and fluting are transformed into lotus flower bulbs.

V-5 THE DECLINE OF THE PORTUGUESE NOBILITY AND THE DISAPPEARANCE OF «GOLDEN GOA'S» PALACES

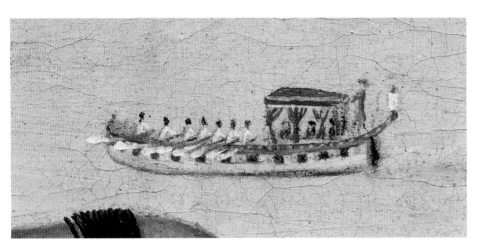

Above. *Type of boat used by the Portuguese nobility for its excursions along the Mandovi River. The painter did not fail to observe the typical black oarsmen from Mozambique. Detail from a painting from the end of the 18th century. Alpoim Galvão Collection*

In the middle of the 17th century, Goa's splendour began to pale. The embassies the Oriental powers had sent to Goa were steadily withdrawn. Powerful foreign traders also left gradually, drawn to the Dutch and English trading posts in places such as Surate or Cochin. The city of Goa was also devastated by huge cholera epidemics, which hastened her decline.

In 1695, the Viceroy Count de Vila Verde abandoned the city and established his residence in Panelim, on Goa's outskirts. He was followed by the archbishop and a large contingent of the nobility.

Panelim was a village on the banks of the Mandovi. The pure, fresh air of the coastal zone, right down to the sea and including the islands of Chorão and Divar, made the whole area the refuge of the lords and rich merchants. There they built their *quintas*. Built as secondary residences, these houses now became their owner's principal dwellings.

Moreover, from 1684 Portuguese settlers increased their efforts to build a new city in Mormugão. This idea, which most of the population did not share, aggravated the dwindling of Goa city's population. The choice of Mormugão was above all supported by the administration in Lisbon, who sent successive viceroys to India with the mandate of pursuing the enormous construction project. But local realities often made them abandon their plans, and the work dragged on slowly. Numerous decrees were published to force populations to move to Mormugão, but the nobility abandoning the capital preferred to set up house in *quintas* in quieter surroundings. In a half-deserted Goa, religious life and festivals remained linked to the city's mythic and sacred places such as the Cathedral of the Good Jesus, which housed the uncorrupted body of Saint Francis Xavier, or the fortress-palace of the viceroys. In the mid-18th century, the situation hadn't improved and the Marquess of Pombal had studies undertaken on the subject of rebuilding a capital in the old city or of building a new one in Pangim. The second alternative was chosen. It was in this zone, then, that the administrative and infrastuctures and port authority were located, as well as the residences of the nobility and merchants.

According to Anquetil du Perron[53], the *quintas* were renovated with materials from the old buildings in Goa city. The author referred notably to the doorways and architectural elements in carved stone which are today

---

[53] **Perron**, Anquetil du, *Zen Avesta*, Paris, 1771, p. 204.

72

found in the buildings of Pangim. As the region of Goa was poor in building materials, it was Bassein, during the city's golden age, which furnished the large pieces of cut stone. The importance and the luxury of these *quintas*, while lacking the splendour of the 17th century buildings, were still marveled at by strangers who described Goa in the 18th century, such and the beginning of the following century, such as Hamilton[54], Edward Ives[55], Visscher[56], Parson[57] and Kloguen[58], this last in the beginning of the 19th century.

Shortly afterwards, Lopes Mendes drew for the pages of his book *Índia portuguesa* the palaces of the Counts of Nova Goa, the Viscounts of Ribandar and the the Viscounts of Carcome Lobo, all nobles who returned to Lisbon and whose houses disappeared or were completely transformed.

While the large palaces were abandoned due to economic crises and cholera epidemics, the *quintas* were abandoned for other motives, more cultural than economic.

Even though Afonso de Albuquerque encouraged marriage between Portuguese and Indians, the more elevated castes continued to refuse to mix their blood with that of foreigners. While these classes assimilated Portuguese culture through education and religious conversion, the notion of purity of blood and the caste system prevented the

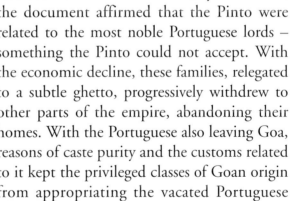

assimilation of noble Portuguese families. As an example of this incompatibility, the Pinto of Candolim sent back the noble title they had received from Lisbon[59] because, by some error, the document affirmed that the Pinto were related to the most noble Portuguese lords – something the Pinto could not accept. With the economic decline, these families, relegated to a subtle ghetto, progressively withdrew to other parts of the empire, abandoning their homes. With the Portuguese also leaving Goa, reasons of caste purity and the customs related to it kept the privileged classes of Goan origin from appropriating the vacated Portuguese palaces, which, for the most part, ended in ruin.

Above. *Plan of the city of Goa during the 17th century,* in Demonstração da Fortaleza de Sofal e das Outras Mais da Índia *by António de Mariz Carneiro. Cod. 149 Biblioteca Nacional. Photo P.C. and C.C.*

[54] **Hamilton**, *op. cit.*, pp. 249-252.

[55] **Ives**, Edward, *A Voyage from England to India*, London, 1773, p. 195.

[56] **Visscher**, Jacob Canter, *Letters from Malabar*, Madras, 1862, p. 32.

[57] **Parson**, Abraham, *Travels in Asia and Africa*, London, 1808, p. 79.

[58] **Kloguen**, *op. cit.*

[59] **Rivara**, J. H. Cunha, *A Conjuração de 1787*, New Goa, 1875, pp. 147-148.

The Consolidation of Power VI

Catholic Bramhin and Chardo Families of the 17th and 18th Centuries

As we have already written, the great Indo-Portuguese architectural legacy which has come down to us was built during the period of decline and impoverishment of the Portuguese empire in the East. The wealth and splendour of these houses show that for their owners, both Brahmin and Chardo families, the situation wasn't the same. The long period of Portuguese decadence coincided, for this elite, with a period of growth in their economic and political power.

If many of their privileges were respected by the Portuguese who arrived in the Indies, from the early 18th century onwards, that protection was extended to their families. Half-abandoned by the Portuguese royal administration which was now focusing its attention on Brazil, the government of Goa found itself needing to rely upon the cultured and lettered classes of the local population. To those classes, on whom it had already conferred many rights, it granted numcrous new advantages, ranks and titles such as *Cavaleiro Fidalgo* («knight-gentleman»), and letters of nobility.

By the end of the 17th century, the Portuguese had already accorded such privileges to Brahmins who had distinguished themselves through loyal services in the Portuguese diplomatic service, administration and tax collection. While these protégés were naturally Brahmins converted to Christianity, members of unconverted Hindu families also participated in the administration, and even in delicate negotiations. In 1613, the viceroy sent Azu Naique to the northern states on a diplomatic mission. Likewise, Crisna Sinai was sent

Previous page. Reception room in the Casa dos Frias in Candolim. Note details of ceiling beams decorated under Hindu inspiration

in 1646 as an envoy to the court of the Sultan of Bijapur. Sinai received special privileges directly from the king of Portugal, including those of living in peace in a Goa under the reproachful eye of the Inquisition.[60]

Chronic corruption in the Portuguese power structure, as well as the complexity of administering property, caused local administrators to transfer tasks to the Christianised Brahmin class, which was known for its ethical and moral behaviour.

For its part, the church concentrated her efforts on converting this class of locals, which could often have as an after effect the conversion of the whole community to Christianity. The religious orders, many of them opposed to the Inquisition, had a determining role in defending the Brahmins' rights – a factor that was a essential to their success in converting the same population. The Brahmins' high spiritual level then permitted some of them to rise to the highest ecclesiastical ranks.[61] Dom Matheus de Castro, a doctor of theology and the first archbishop of Goan origin, was consecrated in 1637. Then in 1702[62], Father António João de Frias published in Lisbon the first

book on Brahmin aristocracy. In it, he defended the nobility of his caste, as well as the services it had rendered both to the government of India and to the evangelisation of Asia and Africa. Such was the case with the Lobo, the Cunha, the Gonçalves, and the Frias families. This last still owns today an early 18th century Indo-Portuguese house that is among the most interesting and best preserved. Pascoal António de Frias, who held many important posts including that of Paymaster General of the Royal treasury, received the title of knight-gentleman by the edict of March 1, 1671. His son José, principal comptroller of the royal treasury, received in 1690 the right to bear a coat of arms for having been Procurator to the queen, that is «*of certain income with which the King favored the Queen for her pocket.*»[63]

In 1712, shortly after Father António de Frias published his defense of the Brahmin nobility, Father Leonardo de Paez was editing a work[64] demonstrating the nobility of the Chardo caste. He laid out the royal lineage of his family, descended from the kings of Sirgapor, and enumerated the services his grandfather had rendered to the Portuguese cause. The church's protection of these castes is clearly due to the fact that these two extremely cultivated religious men were able to defend the lineage of their castes.

Below. View of the façade of the Casa dos Gama in Verna. Photo H. C.

[60] *O Oriente Português*, N.º 5, New Goa, 1933, p. 1.

[61] *Arquidiocese de Goa, op. cit.*

[62] **Frias**, Padre António João de, *Aureola de Indios. Nobiliárquica Brachmane. Tratado Histórico, Geneológico, Panegiro e Moral*, Lisbon, 1702.

[63] **Cunha Rivara**, *op. cit.*, p. 144.

[64] **Paez**, Padre Leonardo de, *Prontuario das Diffinições Indicas*, Lisbon, 1713.

From the middle of the 18th century, the power and social prestige previously accorded to a relatively few individuals became gradually more generalised. The titles of chevalier-gentleman and Knight of the Order of Saint James of the Sword, as well as the right to bear a coat of arms, multiplied. In addition to posts in the Portuguese administration, the creation of an officers' school in Goa allowed its grander families to attain the highest military posts. Aires José Gomes was colonel and field marshal of the province of Salcete in 1817,[65] and he also received the title of Knight of the Order of Saint James.

Goa, seat of Portugal's empire in the Indies, exerted its power from the east coast of Africa to the Far East. Its port developed heavy commerce with the biggest cities in Asia, Africa and Brazil. With the end of the strategic role of the Indies route in the 18th century, and the resulting loss of the Crown's monopoly, Goans were able to develop independent trade with China, Europe and Brazil.

While carried on at a smaller scale than it had been during the 16th and 17th centuries, this trade showed itself to be particularly lucrative. Despite some fluctuations, Goan shipowners and large traders enjoyed prosperous times by taking advantage of the international political situation, especially Napoleon's embargo on English ships. All the British trade coming from the Indies was then carried on Goan ships, and loaded in Goan harbours.[66]

During the first half of the 19th century, the opium trade with China and the British embargo again benefitted Goans, who exported the drug from the region of Malwa towards China. The taxes on this trade, which were collected by Portuguese customs officers, were the most important source of revenue for the remnants of the once great Portuguese empire in India. Christian Brahmins and Chardos became the economic and administrative support which maintained the independence of the Indian state until the second half of the 20th century.

Above. *Detail of the railings of the balconied windows imitating iron balusters. Casa dos Gama in Verna. Photo H. C.*

[65] **Aires Gomes**, Joaquim Manuel, *Biografy of Colonel & Chief-Field Marshal...*, Goa, 1993.

[66] **Pinto**, Celsa, *Goa-Based Overseas and Coastal Trade, 18th and 19th Centuries. In: Goa Through the Ages.* Ed. Teotónio de Sousa, vol. II, pp. 146-175.

VI-1 THE «CHÃ» TRADITION AND THE «CASA DE SOBRADO» IN THE 17TH AND EARLY 18TH CENTURIES

Above and right. *Façade overlooking the gardens and detail of the reception room, Casa dos Gonçalves in Guirim.* Opposite page. *View of the gardens seen from a window of the main floor*

After successive plague epidemics raged through Goa in the 17th century, the Portuguese nobility progressively withdrew to farms in the surrounding countryside or to *quintas* in the outskirts of the city. Wealthy Indian families moved to the provinces of Bardez and Salcete, where they had land or relatives with privileges in their communities.

The Frias from Santana moved to Candolim (Bardez), motivated by their alliance by marriage to the powerful Pinto family. The Mascarenhas, chiefs of the community of Chorão, and later Viscounts of Daman, retired to Anjuna. And the Costa who lived in Ella, in the parish of Goa, went on to Parra. These migrations are still visible today, because the families continue to register their children in the communities from which they originally came, so as to retain their ancient privileges.

In the 17th century, the provinces of Salcete and Bardez were not secure enough to build

large houses in. In 1654 and again in 1659,[67] Adil Shah's troops from Bijapur invaded and pillaged these provinces. In 1667, Bardez was again invaded, this time by the troops of the Maharajah of Sambhaji[68]. In addition, the Rane, a sort of military aristocracy which dominated the regions beyond the borders, made frequent raids on Portuguese territory, looting the dwellings of wealthy land owners.

The Pinto family of Candolim, whose house was already reputed in the 17th century, enjoyed the protection of the fort at Aguada, built on their lands and with their financial participation.

The oldest house examples from the 17th century found in Bardez and Salcete provinces allow us to see that most of them underwent significant enlargements during the 18th and 19th centuries – a period of political stability and of accumulation of wealth for their owners.

Often the presence of a 17th century chapel of ample proportions confirms the existence of privileges and power indicative of economic strength. Nonetheless, the alterations these houses underwent in the late 18th and early 19th centuries render the historic analysis of these buildings difficult.

In the cases where we can see older construction, Portuguese norms are present. The chapel, which later would be integrated in the house's interior in the same way as a family altar in a Hindu house, is still independent and located on a plaza or a courtyard of Portuguese conception. The Pinto and Monteiro houses in Candolim, the Costa house in parra, the Piedade Costa house in Majorda, and the Machado house at Nagoa are all examples of

[67] **Souza**, Teotónio de, *Goa Medieval – A Cidade e o Interior no Século XVII*, Lisbon, Ed. Estampa, 1994, p. 35.
[68] **Souza**, Teotónio de, *op. cit.*, p. 42.

Above and right. *Façade, detail of the main entrance and plan of the main floor of the Casa dos Pintos in Arporá*

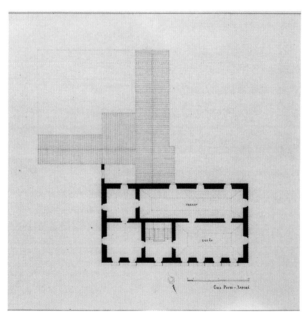

groupings which include a large 17th century or early 18th century chapel built independently on its own ground. The Machado house, since fundamentally altered, still shows the vestiges of a highly-decorated, colonnaded balcony and stucco work on some windows of clear 17th century inspiration. A large entry portal opening in the courtyard wall reminds one of descriptions of the viceroys' and archbishops' palaces in Goa.

In the Piedade Costa house in Majorda, the Pinto house in Santa Cruz and the Gama family house in Verna , all of which are examples of 17th and early 18th century construction, the simple volumes on two floors as described by Ramponi[69] reveal a tendency towards plane architecture, and to the pure, refined style of the 17th century. None of these edifices have an entryway directly on to the street; entry is reached by a lateral flight of steps linked to the courtyard. Yet, even while these houses were so close to the colonial norms of architecture, each was also endowed with a healthy portion of Hindu tradition in the form of a long, narrow *vasary*.

Unlike the colonial houses where the nobles lived on the upper floor and the servants on the ground floor, the servants in these houses belonging to the privileged Indian classes lived completely separately from their masters. Among the *casa de sobrado*, a few examples retained their «chã» aesthetic throughout the 18th century. If some of these houses were built or restored during the first half of the century, others integrated baroque elements introduced during the 18th century and conserved until the 19th century.

The interior layout of these houses is characterised by a lateral entrance almost inde-

Left. *Chapel of Saint Sebastian founded by the Pintos of Arporá on land in front of their house. Above the main entrance, the arms of the Pintos*

pendent of the house's main structure. The staircase is treated in secondary fashion, without being an organising factor for the interior rooms. Neither does it possess the monumental quality that baroque architecture conferred on staircases, such as those in the Santana da Silva palace, the Miranda house in Margão, or the Bragança house in Chandor.

---

[69] **Ramponi**, *op. cit.*, pp. 300-301.

In «chã» architecture, the entry way is used as a tool to separate the interior and exterior spaces, between the sacred and the profane. The walled courtyard with a large portal, as in the archbishops' palace in Goa, reinforces this separation. The courtyard established a transitional space between the dwelling's exterior and interior, and made domestic life sacred. While this sacred space is more clear in 17th century houses, it is still evident in the Gonçalvez house in Guirim and those of the Gama family at Saligão and the Miranda family at Loutulim. In the Gonçalvez house, the entry door reveals baroque tastes, but the spirit of the formal structure is that of «chã» architectonic concepts.

In this group of buildings, the design of the façade is more austere, with spare decoration, the pilasters playing a less important role in the composition. In the cases where 17th century Italian Mannerist influence is present, the pilasters alternate in rhythmic fashion as in the Miranda house in Loutulim, but they are simply designed, without fluting or carving work. In the Pinto house in Santa Cruz, however, the eaves are embellished with denticles in the Mannerist tradition is without equal in Portugal.

Window decoration is generally unremarkable, consisting merely of the window frames. As for the balconies, the most common design is composed of three brackets characteristic of the 17th century, which remained in use until the 18th century. In the Gonçalvez house in Guirim, the simply bracketed balconies resemble those in the Palace of Archbishops. The house's wooden balustrades, even though typical of the 17th and 18th centuries, have practically disappeared. Over the course of the 19th century, their pure lines were replaced by the more elaborate designs of romantic grillwork.

The importance of proportions and the specific characteristics of the Miranda house make it the most significant example of this type of dwelling. Built during the first half of the 18th century, and modified during the following century, the principal façade's design shows that this habitation is the fruit of adapting a type of house with the lateral entry way, as was the case with the Piedade Costa house in Majorda. The entrance is almost imperceptible, hidden in the series of window-doors on the ground floor. Only the house's coat of arms placed above the door signals it as an entrance. The simple molding on the pilasters which, alternating with rectangular windows, span the façade, as well as the balconies' pure lines, are the expression of a 17th century aesthetic.

The staircase has secondary importance in the internal structure of these buildings. Placed in the corner of a room it is conceived as a simple, functional element without an aesthetic or stage-setting role.

CASA PIEDADE COSTA MAJORDA

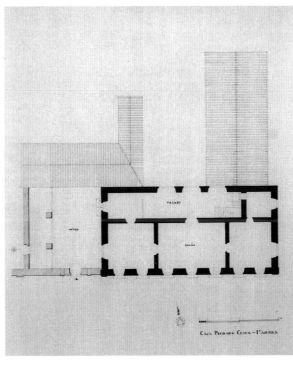

CASA PIEDADE COSTA – MAJORDA

T he unity of the different buildings which constitute this ensemble make this house one of the most interesting examples of the «chã» architectural tradition in Goa.

Surrounded by palm trees, the house is situated on a large city square. The chapel, which underwent numerous restorations but which retained its original characteristics, is also of large proportions. Its nave, covered by a coffered vault, is, even in its smallest details, of a quality and attention rare in a private house. The sacristy houses an altar, apparently from the 17th century and apparently original to the building. Between the chapel and the outdoor stone cross is a large well which fed water to the house.

According to Portuguese tradition, entry to the house was achieved through the lateral

Above and left. *Elevation and plan of the main floor of the Casa dos Piedade Costa in Majorda. The chapel of the house invoking Nossa Senhora da Piedade would give the name Piedade to the Costas of Majorda, in Goan nobility's tradition.*
Survey by At. H. C.

court, creating an intermediate space and a clear break between exterior and interior. It was in this part of the house that the women descended from their litter without being seen from the outside. In the case of the Piedade Costa house, this courtyard also linked the house with the chapel.

But the most interesting aspect of this house is doubtless the autonomy of the family's apartments vis-a-vis the servants' quarters. Even though the house is built on two storeys in European tradition, the fact that Indian rules forbade servants of low castes any access to their master's quarters meant that the ground floor had to be organised in two wings, with the boundary between them clearly defined. Despite its external appearance of Portuguese tradition, the codes of domestic life inside were purely Hindu. On the upper floor, the salon was reserved for exceptional events, taking on the role of the *sadery*, while the ground floor was reserved for daily activities.

Left and below. Of great significance in terms of heritage, the architectural complex that makes up the Casa dos Piedade Costa keeps to the original layout with a square and chapel, a large cross and a well. The entrance to the house is still through the side patio in 17th century tradition

Right. *Main entrance crowned by the coat of arms of the family. Casa dos Rosário Miranda in Loutulim*

Like Candolim, Loutulim is a Brahmin village, which explains the existence of grand houses in both towns. If Candolim benefitted from the protection of the Aguada fortress, Loutulim was protected by the fortress in Rachol, and under the influence of the Jesuit fathers. While far from Goa, its situation near the banks of the Zuari River, the conduit for much commercial traffic towards the interior of Salcete province, facilitated access to the capital.

Among the grand houses of Loutulim, the Miranda house reveals specific characteristics which make it a magnificent example of the 17th century prior to the baroque period. Its vast proportions and its complex layout bear witness to the growing power of this Brahmin family, parallel to the decline of the Portuguese nobility. The family retained its power until the 19th century, when Constâncio do Rosário e Miranda received the title of knight-gentleman and letters of nobility from the royal house.

The structure and formal composition of the house, whose appearance is sobre and massive, are near to the «chã» aesthetic of the palaces of Portuguese nobles. Even though they were Brahmins, the Mirandas distinguished themselves in the army and in combat against the Rane who dominated the provinces of Pondá near Loutulim, on the opposite shores of the Zuari. Perhaps this military experience explains the solemnity of the two-storey façade and its severe design, with simply framed windows. The entrance, built along the 17th century canons, is lateral, and is made through a

Above and left. *Drawing of the main façade of the house and detail of the study with an 18th century Indo-Portuguese chair*

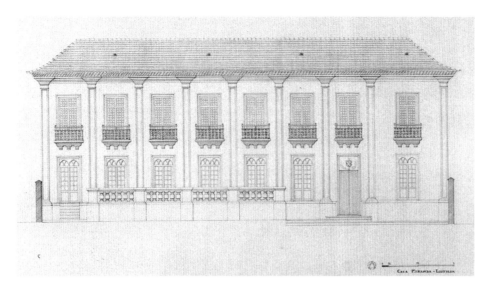

floor. The upper floor, consisting of a *sadery* and guest rooms as in Hindu houses, does not play the role of the first floor. The chapel room, which clearly fulfills the functions of a *vasary*, is another aspect of Hindu tradition. It is situated between the living rooms and the kitchen area, thereby playing more of the role of a *vasary* than of a chapel.

The characteristics of this interior structure indicate that the current house is the result of transformation of an old house based on traditional Hindu dwelling compositions. This hypothesis is reinforced by the existence of a central courtyard, on which open the large living room and a gallery whose ambiance evokes the Hindu *raj angan*.

Finally, this house has a small garden which, as in the dean's palace, is one of the last examples of Portuguese tradition which Indians did not adapt and preserve in their houses. Nearly all the travelers who wrote about Goa during the 17th and 18th centuries referred to gardens surrounded by high walls with *«cisterns and fish ponds to bathe in, in which they take great pleasure..»*[70] The garden is organised in two small allées with a lake at their intersection, and vases posed on pedestals the length of the garden paths. At the end of one of the allées is a belvedere with a small wall, which must have been part of a shady pavilion like that at the dean's palace.

Above and right. Main elevation and plan of the ground floor of the Casa dos Rosário Miranda in Loutulim. Survey by At. H. C. Next page. *View of the room which gives on to the interior patio of the house. A palanquin hangs from one of the roof trusses. It was a type of litter used in Goa until the 19th century.*

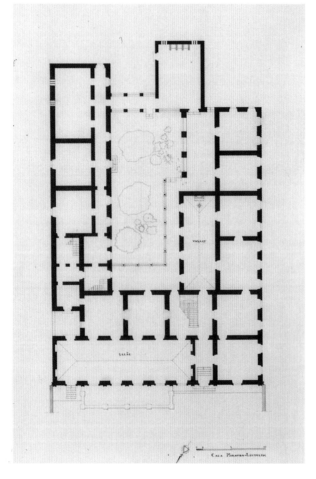

window-door. Even the staircases leading to the upper floor reach only so far as a transition room, as if there were patched on.

As in other houses described in this book, the living quarters are mostly on the ground

[70] **Linschoten**, *op. cit.*, p. 70.

THE SPLENDOUR OF THE PINTO FAMILY VII

AND THE PÁTIO HOUSE STYLE IN BARDEZ AND SALCETE

It is without doubt the hegemony of the Pinto family of Candolim that gave Bardez province the *casa de pátio* house type during the first half of the 18th century.

This style, more in conformity with Hindu customs and habit, is the result of the adaptation from the 16th century on of the houses of converted Brahmins and Chardos. The symbolic force of the *casa de sobrado* during Portuguese supremacy in the 16th and into the 17th century was surely responsible for overshadowing the *casa de pátio* style. But the latter came back into favour during the 18th century. And even Portuguese settlers would use the *pátio* style to great advantage for their country houses.

This change in influence explains the refined design of the Monteiro house in Candolim, where a Mannerist influence is clearly manifest on the façade and in the interior structure.

Above and left. *Drawing of the Casa dos Costa Frias in Candolim and detail of the façade, emphasising the elaborate stucco work on the windows and pilasters*

91

Right. *Appoach to and detail of the entrance to the Casa dos Costa Martins in Assolna. Built with screened windows, the entrance door is finished off with in a peacock tail, a decorative feature in Hindu tradition*

This type of house, doubtless inspired by the now-vanished Pinto palace, was developed in this area with a group of 18th century houses whose aesthetic affinities show a common reference model.

These houses are characterised, in addition to their arrangements around central court-yards (*pátios*), by the very rich ornamentation of their façades, walls and entry stairs. The front door itself is included in a high wall enclosing the house. This characteristic is even more present during the 19th century and in middle-class houses of the first half of the 20th century, which revived the taste for elaborate stucco work in balustrades, vases, flames and other decorative elements.

The most interesting example, however, is the Frias house, which we will analyse on its own in another chapter. The façade design reveals a taste for the Italian Mannerist style,

like that of the Monteiro house, to which are added several notes of baroque grammar.

The Campos family house in Calangute is another very interesting example. As in the Frias house, the ceilings have chevrons in carved wood, as in the civil architecture of the 16th century. At one end of the main beam is inscribed «Made on», and at the other end, «19 Dec. 1746.» With its small dimensions, this house has similarities to the Frias house, both in the size of its foundations and in the design of the façade, embellished only with fluted pilasters on the ground floor and double pilasters on the corners of the second floor. The entrance porch is clearly of a later period. The construction date allows us to situate this house style more generally in the first half of the 18th century.

Another house in Anjuna, also belonging to the Frias family but dating to the end of the

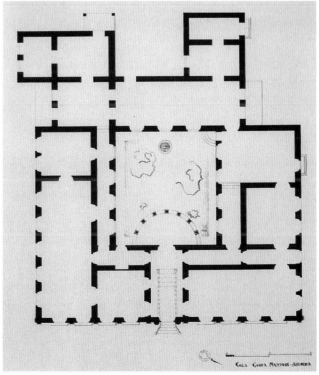

Above and left. *Displaying 17th century architectural features in its interior this patio house clearly suggests an evolution of this architectural style begining with the Hindu patio house. Main façade and plan of the ground floor of the Casa dos Costa Martins in Assolna. Survey by At. H. C.*

18th century, has a strange porch – as if the former doorway had been moved back to find itself right in front of the porch.

In Salcete, there are two *casa de sobrado* which seem to date from the 17th century: the Casa dos Costa Martins in Assolna, and the Casa do Alemão in Betalbatim. The first has, inside, vestiges of pilasters with classical angel decorations on its capitals. These pilasters corresponded with an older façade of the house which had been incorporated to the interior when the building was enlarged. The later works were, judging by their decorative grammar, done in the 18th century. The house's furnishings include four lovely arm chairs dated 1674, which show the importance of this dwelling as early as the 17th century.

From available documentation and from Brahmin and Chardo houses still existent, the use of Portuguese-influenced furniture became progressively more common during the 18th century, because the Hindus were usually happier with small objects that were easily portable around the interior.

In the Casa do Alemão, there is a wing next to the chapel which has classical pilasters of hewn stone, rare in Goa where laterite was the only stone commonly found. Between the pilasters are cut large round windows cased in mother of pearl, the *carepas*, whose design is reminiscent of the galleries of Goa's 17th century colonial architecture. During the second half of the following century, to follow the style of the grand palaces, this house was

expanded with a new façade adjoining the rear of the chapel, which then became the new core of the edifice.

As in these two examples, other cases present older structures more difficult to date. The stability of these families, whose rights and property was generally preserved by the Portuguese from the 16th century onwards, allowed several of these houses to stay in a single family for centuries, with their cores predating the arrival of Europeans in Goa.

Above. *Together with the Casa dos Costa Martins in Assolna, the Casa dos Teotónio Alemão in Betalbatim displays architectural features dating from the 16th and 17th centuries. Detail of the rear of the chapel seen from the entrance porch.*

Previous page. *View of the reception room in the Casa dos Costa Martins in Assolna. In the foreground two armchairs dated 1674*

95

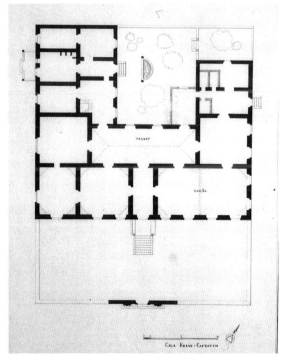

Above and left. *Elevation and plan of the Casa dos Costa Frias in Candolim. Survey by At. H. C.*

Previous page. *Entrance gate to the garden*

Like the Monteiro family residence, this house is an example of architecture highly influenced by the Italian Mannerist style, even though it was built at the beginning of the 18th century. More than in the Monteiro house, this one was erected under the protection of the Pinto family. The Frias already had a great deal of prestige during the 17th century, often holding the highest posts in the Goan administration. The decline of the empire and the cholera epidemics motivated the Frias family to leave its house in Santana de Talaulim, in the outskirts of Goa, and to resettle in Candolim. In the beginning of the 18th century, Simão Salvador de Frias, the only son of Caetano de Frias, settled in part of his maternal grandfather Simão Pinto's house. The Frias house is situated in this part, which had been the Pinto family's original

Above. Wash basin in the dining room of the Casa dos Costa Frias in Candolim. The great aesthetic quality of this piece and its 17th century design is an example of this families' taste and financial power already during the 17th century

palace, and which became Frias property when set apart by Simão Salvador de Frias' widow.

From this house of refined proportions emanates a sophisticated Mannerist spirit mixed with an eastern baroque ornamental grammar, which can also be found in the old chapel of the Pinto house, nearby.

The alternating pilasters and windows are present here, too, as they are in the Monteiro house, but the pilaster capitals are less elaborate. The same is true of the double pilasters which punctuate the corners of the upper floor, an erudite detail that we also find on the Monteiro's house. The new baroque grammar is used on window frames, and notably in the scrolls, which we can also admire in the churches of Calangute and Assagão.

Following Portuguese tradition, the entrance is preceded by a court surrounded by a high wall as in the archbishops' palace. A portal of large proportions is cut into the surrounding wall, framed by Corinthian columns and topped by pinnacles and a pediment bearing a niche and a cross. This refined design shows affinities with religious architecture.

Not far from that, at Nerul, the Augustinian fathers had owned, since the 17th century, a country *quinta* which today is the property of the Lopes family. While much modified since, it has conserved a magnificent portal resembling that of the Frias house, which confirms the interaction of civil and religious architecture.

A porch signals the Frias' entrance; its form corresponds to the typical model which became common during the 19th century, but here it is a precursor for that later fashion.

Like the porch, the interior structure is also of a configuration that became popular in 19th century houses. The flight of steps leading up to the porch continues on to become a small hallway leading onto the living rooms and the *vasary*. In the entertaining rooms the ceiling beams are carved in Hindu fashion, and on the

Left. *Detail of the screened windows and room with ceiling girders with Hindu decoration. Casa dos Costa Frias in Candolim*

central beam of the living room is engraved the family's crest. The coat of arms was bestowed in 1690 on Pascoal de Frias, grandfather of the builder of this house. Because it was a rare distinction at the time, it was natural that the Frias would want to show it off. The dining room has a curious but very beautiful marble basin in the center, for washing hands before and after meals. Its Mannerist design is quite a bit older than the house, which must mean that it was brought here from the Frias' former house in Santana de Talaulim.

QUINTAS IN 18ᵀᴴ CENTURY PANGIM VIII

AND THE INTRODUCTION
OF THE BAROQUE AESTHETIC

Like a last, autumnal flowering on the banks of the Mandovi, a significant number of *quintas* and palaces were scattered on Indian soil as late as the 18th and 19th centuries, built by the Portuguese nobility.

From the second half of the 18th century on, new styles copied from Lisbon and baroque architectural concepts appeared with greater frequency in these large houses.

This aesthetic, which brought with it a new decorative grammar, also introduced a new façade style, with a symmetrical scheme built out from the centre, signaled by a main entryway with a tribune-style balcony above it on the first floor, the balcony in turn capped by a triangular pediment at roof level. The entryway was linked to an internal core of stairways, which now became the organising element of the house's internal structure. A new relationship was established between the externally visible structure and the organisation of the interior; the façade would from now on translate outwards the house's internal logic. The large entry door hereby lost the preeminent and independent role it had occupied during the 16th and 17th centuries and became integrated in the façade, which became more important as a whole.

Though without the pomp of 17th century *quintas*, the quality of these houses – the last vestiges of an age already past – was enough to be remarked upon by foreign travelers visiting Goa.

From Parson, who arrived for a stay in 1776, to Forbes or the Abbot Cottineau de Klon-

Previous page.
Detail of the door of the main façade of the Palácio dos Santana da Silva in Margão. Photo H. C.

Above. *Palácio dos Condes de Nova Goa in Pangim. The pediment over the entrance reveals clear affinities with the pediment on the main façade of the Palácio dos Bragança in Chandor. Drawing by Lopes Mendes from his book* Índia Portuguesa

guen, who were here in the early 19th century, everyone spoke of the city's state of ruin, which had not yet encompassed the religious edifices or the farms and palaces along the Mandovi. Kloguen wrote in 1823: «*Someone coming from Pangim, seeing in the distance the number of churches in Goa, with their steeples and bell towers, and the magnificent houses of Panelim, could truly believe he was entering a superb metropolis.*»[71]

These *quintas* were mostly concentrated in the area of Pangim, closer to the sea and in the wake of successive dwellings of viceroys. Abandoning the Casa da Pólvora palace in Panelim, the Count of Ega installed himself in the Pangim palace in 1759. This former fortress of Adil Shah had been restored in order to become a country residence for viceroys. During the first half of the 18th century, they lived in this *quinta* before officially taking their posts, or after leaving it while waiting for the ship that would carry them back to Lisbon.[72] Following the viceroy's example, the arch-

bishop moved into a country palace he already owned in this area, in Santa Inês, abandoning his palace in Panelim. This *quinta* had been given in 1736 by the Canon Francisco da Cunha Souto-Mayor, the last descendant in India of one of the most important 17th century Portuguese families: the Sottomayor.[73]

A few large houses remained in Ribandar, such as the palaces of the Carcome Lobo family and the Viscounts of Ribandar, but most of the grand families remained concentrated in Pangim during the 18th century.

A survey of the Pangim and Santa Inês area, conducted during the 18th century under orders from the governor Dom José Pedro da Câmara (1774-1779), described a vast group of large farms along the Mandovi's banks, surrounded by pretty gardens in the European taste. These *quintas*, by their distribution, evoke images of the farms along the Tagus River from Santos to Belém and which were inventoried by Carlos Mardel before the earthquake of 1755.

The survey map notes the owners of these palaces, which are now destroyed or entirely altered. Most are families who would later leave India, such as the Counts of Nova Goa, the Melo Sampaio, the Almeida and the Melo families.

Even though they are for the most part destroyed now, it was these *quintas* which heralded the apparition of baroque concepts in Brahmin and Chardo family houses. The houses of important local families would now begin to gain in importance over those of Portuguese families.

The pediment, a polarising element for the first floor, was common in Portugal during the first half of the 18th century, notably in palaces

[71] **Kloguen**, *op. cit.*, p. 82.

[72] *Relação da Viagem que... fizeram à Índia... os Marqueses de Távora*, Lisbon, 1752, p. 237.

[73] *Memória Histórica-Eclesiástica da Arquidiocese de Goa*, Ed. Amaro Pinto Lobo, New Goa, 1933, p. 146.

such as those of the Marquess of Abrantes, of Sousa Mexia on the Campo Grande, or the Palácio do Mindelo. This pediment appears to be a new element underlining the building's spatial continuity and emphasising the frontal approach of the façade.

The pediment defined a tripartite division by creating two symmetrical wings, which gave the whole structure a more dramatic impact when seen from a distance. The path leading to the house was prolonged naturally by the central doorway, which gave access to the vestibule and then to the stairway which penetrated the house. This scheme was used in the Bragança palace at Chandor. It had been experimented with previously in palaces such as those of the Melo Sampaios, the Counts of Nova Goa in Pangim, and the Viscounts of Ribandar.

Old documentation helps in the analysis of the aesthetic changes of these palaces, now disappeared, and the paintings in the Alpoim Galvão collection that show the mouth of the Mandovi River are precious in this regard. By looking at these canvases, along with some drawings by Lopes Mendes and some 19th century photographs by Paul and De Sousa, it is possible to define some of the changes in the

most important reference models. We can see, for instance, that the triangular pediment marking the principal façade of the palace of the Counts of Nova Goa is similar to that of the Bragança palace in Chandor. The central doorway structure and the design of the lateral façade also has affinities with those of Santana da Silva palace in Margão.

Outside the Goa area, in the remote province of Quepém, the Palácio do Deão (Dean's palace) still stands. Here the features of Baroque aesthetics are present inside as well as out. Stretching lengthways, the façade presents a tripartite design with a central section crowned by a pediment on which are carved the arms of the prelate. Built as a country house, the palace consists of only one floor. To give it greater dignity, the building rises from a raised platform from which an enormous staircase descends to the entrance courtyard. It is interesting to note that the façade is decorated with alternating pilasters and balconied windows, and double pilasters at the corners, clearly showing that the Mannerist tradition continued to be in use during this century.

The exterior spaces at the rear and sides of the palace – galleries and covered verandas used for relaxation – are also of enormous

Above. *View of the town of Ribandar on the outskirts of the city of Goa where most of the grand houses of the Portuguese nobility during the 17th and 18th centuries were concentrated. Detail from a painting of the end of the 18th century. Alpoim Galvão Collection*

103

historical value. These galleries, along with the fountains and pavilions in the garden, confirm written descriptions of other palaces no longer extant that were built with greater financial means.

The chapel, just in front of the house's entrance, shows Hindu influence for which no equivalent is found in Portugal. The chapel opens out onto the house's entrance and its large porch, which allowed worshipers to sit on the house porch and stairway during the celebration of mass. They were seated, of course, in strict hierarchical order on the stairs and landings, in accordance with caste distinction.

The Santana da Silva palace in Margão and other less imposing examples, like those of the Miranda family in Margão and the Osório Saldanha family in Arossim, also belong to the same class of house.

While the baroque aesthetic pervaded a certain number of buildings, it only had a fleeting influence on the evolution of civilian architecture built by Brahmin and Chardo families. As we have said, these families preferred a single-storey dwelling to the creation of a first floor above a ground floor reserved for servants.

But it was also just at this period that some Brahmin and Chardo families began to be

PEDRO

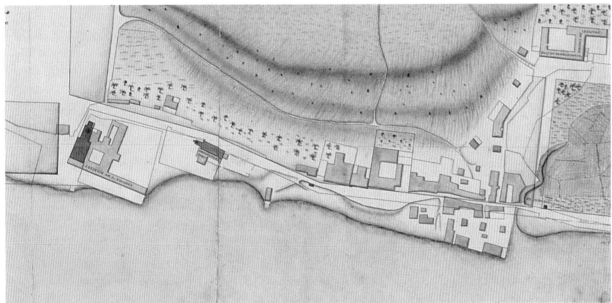

Above. *São Pedro, on the outskirts of the city with the Palácio dos Cárcome Lobo standing out at the centre from amongst the architectural frontage of grand houses. Detail from a painting of the end of the 18th century. Alpoim Galvão Collection.*
Left. *Plan of the São Pedro area, still showing the location of various palaces which have disappeared completely. Plan from the second half of the 18th century. Gabinete de Estudos Históricos de Fortificação e Obras Militares*

interested in the representative value of their houses, and more precisely of the monumental nature of the façade. The façade, therefore, became progressively longer, and the most surprising example of this is the Bragança palace in Chandor.

R I O   D E   G O A

THE PALÁCIO DOS MELO DE SAMPAIO   VIII-1
IN SANTA INÊS

This palace, situated on the outskirts of Pangim, was built by the Melo Sampaios during the mid-18th century. The occupation of Bassein by the Maratas in 1739 forced the family to retire to Goa. Although they lost the enormous properties they owned in Baçaim, the Melo Sampaios quickly regained their importance and wealth. After the disaster of Bassein, Goa expanded its territories towards the middle of the 18th century through successive campaigns against the Maratas. The Portuguese extended their frontiers by annexing several provinces which became known as the Novas Conquistas (new conquests).

A peace treaty finally signed with the Maratas in 1759, and the accompanying income and taxes from the new territories, gave some financial respite to the small population of Portuguese aristocracy living in India. Thanks to their role as active military leaders during the campaigns, the Melo Sampaios recovered wealth which, if not equal to the splendour in which they had lived before 1739, was enough to build a palace in keeping with the fashionable standards of the late baroque which had crossed the Atlantic and Indian Oceans to reach India.

Already completely in ruins by the middle of the 19th century, this house was described at the time by one of its last residents: João de Melo de Sampaio. His description is particulary important, as it refers to a layout and style that was typical to palaces built by Portuguese nobility in India but which had disappeared almost entirely by the early 20th cen-

tury. The description, which predates major alterations undertaken on the palace to bring it up to date in 19th century style, makes it all the more important as a document of the cross pollenation of influence in architectural styles developed by the Portuguese and by the Christian Brahmin and Chardo families.

The description confirms many of the feature of an Indo-Portuguese house. The chapel, inside the house, is situated «*on the first floor, in the most intimate heart of this two-storey house.*» The importance of verandas and galleries extending along various wings of the building, allowing air circulation, is also described:

«*It is a big house, tall, with two gardens and a central portico at the front, in the village of Santa Inês. Inside the first floor, within the heart of this two-storey house, there was a chapel where Mass was celebrated on an altar decorated with a beautiful reredos. There were six teak columns artistically carved that coiled in spirals from the pedestal to the capital.*

«*This was the family's sanctuary, and in the centre of this colonnade a statue of Our Lady of Remédios was placed to serve as patron saint and protectress. The statue had been brought from Goa among the precious items which the Melo de Sampaio family had been forced to bring from Bassein, where they lived in a house with a chapel, when, in 1739, the Maratas, under orders from the Baji Rao, occupied the city.*» (Among these items might also have been the famous East India Company dinner service which is now dispersed throughout the world but of

Above. *Pangim urban complex with the Palácio dos Noronha, no longer standing, on the extreme left.*

Right. *Detail of a list with all the names of the owners of the most important houses in the area during the second half of the 18th century. Gabinete de Estudos Históricos de Fortificação e Obras Militares*

Relação dos Edifficios e cazas nobres, e mais concideraveis, que todas vaõ apro- veitadas, e contempladas neste projecto.

A Palacio de Jllma. e Exmo Snr Governador, e Capp.am Genr.l
B Palacio do Exmo. e Rmo. Snr. Arcepispo Primáz.
C Freguezia de N. Sr.a da Conceição de Pangim.
D Freguezia de Sta. Jgnêz.
E Cazas q. foraõ do Brigadeiro D. Antonio de Noronha.
F Quartel da companhia de Cavallos.
G Cazas de D. Rodrigo de Castro.
H Cazas q. foraõ de Joze Placido de Mattos Saraiva.
I Cazas de Paschoal Henriques.
L Cazas de Joaquim Caetano Suares.
M Cazas de D. Manoel Antonio de Almeida.
N Cazas de Antonio de Amaral.
O Cazas de Francisco da Costa Maquinés.
P Cazas de Caetano Xavier de Aguiar.
Q Cazas de Valentim da Costa Campos.
R Cazas de Joaõ Gomes da Costa.
S Cazas de D. Loppo Joze de Almeida.
T Cazas de Joaõ Vicente da Silveira.
V Cazas de Nicolao Manoel Coelho.
X Cazas de Luiz Xavier.
Z Cazas do Morgade de Sta. Jgnéz em q. se acha aquartelado parte do Regimento de Artelharia.

Todas as Cazas q. neste projecto naõ vaõ netadas se po- dem ver na outra planta, na qual se mostra serem muito pouco concideraveis.

which some superb pieces may be seen in the Museu Nacional de Arte Antiga in Lisbon.)

«*The front of the new chapel in Santa Inês gave onto an entrance which was called the balcony, with a large window in the middle of the façade that looked down onto the Mandovi River. The right-hand side of the chapel opened onto a wide hallway from which one could descend five steps into a living room whose floor was particularly high. To the left, a door with no glass panes or lattice work and no steps, opened into the wardrobe room, which was as wide as the living room and even longer. This vestry room had four wide, tall windows, with comfortable seats, so that two people could fit comfortably in the middle.*

«*On the wall opposite from the windows, a narrow door led into the câmara tabuado (room with wooden planked floor),* and through an

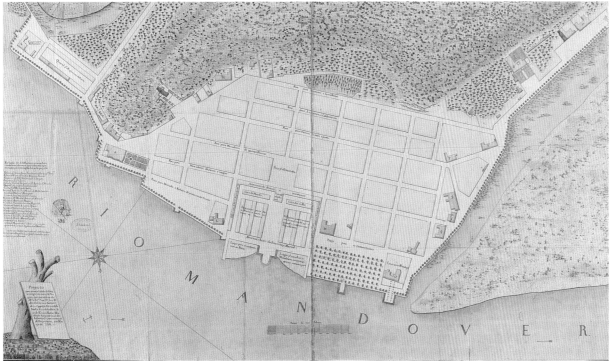

Above. *Group of country estates in the Santa Inês area of Pangim. On the right, the Palácio dos Maquinés. Detail from a painting of the end of the 18th century. Alpoim Galvão Collection*

Left. *Urban project from the Pombaline period foreseeing the integration of the most important country estates and palaces of the region within the new design. Plan dated 1776. Gabinete de Estudos Históricos de Fortificação e Obras Militares*

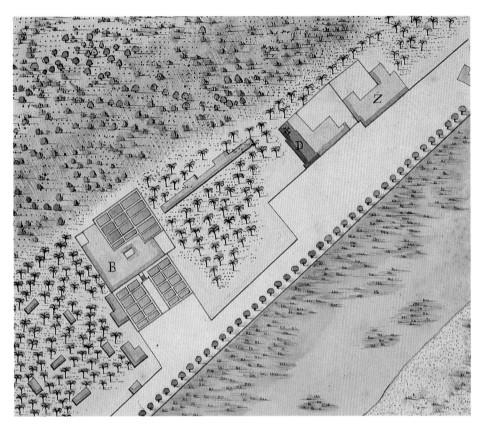

«These rooms were formed large veranda whose exterior wall, open through a series of arches, started at this door and was perpendicular to the dining room. On the other wall, on the Pangim side, there were five communicating doors to the girls' bedrooms, the pantry, the kitchen and two wash rooms, each with a window onto the grove. On the side wall at the end of the veranda, there was only one grilled window looking onto the grove from which one could see the Santa Inês stream, which, passing behind and on the left side of the house, ran underneath the previously mentioned bridge and, following its course under three more bridges, joins the Mandovi next to the present-day hospital. This used to be the old house that had belonged to Diogo and José da Costa de Ataíde e Teive, and was called 'dos Maquineses'.

«The house's cutter or sloop was moored beneath the veranda, and on its bow it bore the family crest. The crew was composed of six negroes. Underneath the five service areas were the storage rooms, where they kept the wood and salt, and where the six oarsmen also slept.

«The main bedroom area had three rooms which were used by the parents and uncles of the author, when they were young and still students.

«The rooms beneath the wardrobe room had windows looking onto the garden on the left, by whose wall was a stone table where tea was prepared for the grandparents in China cups when they awoke from their afternoon naps. The rooms were used by Ricardo and Cristóvão de Melo de Sampaio, second and third born. Francisco de Melo de Sampaio, fourth son of the author's grandfather, had his room next to that of the author's father.

«Beneath the entrance balcony was a masonry arch which supported the biggest part of the staircase. This arch led to the boys' rooms and to where the black nightwatchman slept near the door. The stairway climbed in right angles, the last flight of twenty-two steps reached the balcony, with the landing of the second flight remaining

open door in each of these rooms one passed into a large gallery overlooking the cultivated fields which extended as far as the João de Melo Bridge.

«On the Pangim side, beyond the living room, came the large chambers, the quarters belonging to General de Melo de Sampaio's grandfather. On the same side after the câmara tabuado and behind the chapel was a small room where Dona Branca de Melo slept. She married a first-lieutenant in the artillery, José de Sousa Sepúlveda, who had settled in Santa Inês. The next room was spacious – the same size as the hall – which was the dining room. Beyond that was the grandmother's room which had, high up on the wall, a large crucifix.

«The dining room had two windows which looked onto a grove of palm trees. Between the windows was a space with a three-sided table which could easily seat twelve people. At the end of the wall, and next to the grandmother's bedroom, there was a door leading to the inside rooms and the service area.

just beneath the chapel. The chapel floor was supported by strong beams, and anyone who entered the house had to pass beneath the chapel, but its height was calculated so as not to hinder the passage of heavy loads. This arrangement appears to have been standard throughout the house. The boat was kept by the wide lower entrance, and was moved by the same six negroes who were also the oarsmen and who also carried the litters.

«Beneath the great hall was the cellar for rice and wheat, which had a window onto the garden on the right. Other servants slept in the other store rooms.

«Excess furniture from the neighbouring house of the Pereiras Pintos was kept in the store room beneath the câmara tabuado. The author's grandmother had been the last and only heir of the Pereira Pintos. Among the furniture there were some beautiful chests of drawers in whose drawers one would often find forgotten coins or other items of gold.

«Such was the house of the Melos de Sampaio in Santa Inês. At that time, Portugal, if it did not completely dominate as it had before, was still respected and unrivaled throughout the seas and the lands of the East. The Goan Royal Navy was distinct from the Navy in Portugal, and the profoundly rooted Portuguese presence in India gave a strong sense of security and respect to that dominion, and constituted the greatness and splendour of Portugal in this region.

«In the house at Santa Inês, the family would kneel to pray together in front of the opening on the right-hand side of the chapel, which was reached from the side by a small stairway of five steps.

«On certain days, after prayers, one of the favorite or most familiar of the Creoles would ask the lady of the house for permission to take part in some merry-making, which consisted of singing some appropriate melodies to which they added verses they had invented. They were accompanied by a loud and monotonous playing of a simple beat, played by a servant boy. Each one of the girls who partook in the merry-making was obliged to sing a verse, which more often than not was of her own making and referred to a hint or a taunt.

«On feast days and on certain anniversaries, families who were close to the Melos de Sampaio, or of the same rank, were invited and after tea had been served, followed later by sweetmeats and fine wines, the ladies and pretty girls present would be invited to liven up the party by adding their harmonies to those of the harps and violas. The most talented singers would enchant everyone with their vibrant voices, singing from their bosoms melodies and popular songs with spirited verses, which even today are appreciated and reputed for their quality.

«On such days, while the ladies shined in the salons, the staff would entertain itself with the merry-making already described, to which was added a mandó which the black girls danced at the end....»

Above. *Coat of Arms of the Correa da Silva family in Caranzalem, where this family possessed vast estates. Photo H. C.*

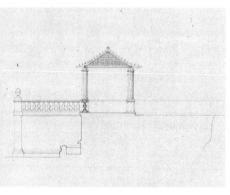

Above. *Main elevation of the Palácio do Deão in Quepém, showing the group of verandas and garden loggias. Survey by At. H. C.*

Given that almost all Portuguese civilian architecture has disappeared, this edifice is of great importance for analysing Indo-Portuguese house types. Its garden, though now in total in ruin, still retains some features, such as the pond, the open air loggia, the belvedere, balustrades, vases and stone ornaments, which furnish us with information on a complex garden quite unparalleled in Goa outside descriptions of the oldest palaces.

Father José Paulo da Costa Pereira de Almeida, who arrived in India in 1780 as a parson in Archbishop Dom Fr. Manuel de Santa Catarina's entourage, and who was afterwards made Dean, was responsible for the start of construction on the palace, around 1787. This was also the starting date for construction on the Santa Cruz church. The date is etched in a stone plaque on the cross in the churchyard.

In his will, the Dean endowed the palace as a country estate for the Viceroys: «*leisure only for the vacations they may wish to spend there, without being able to have the entire use of these houses.*»[74] The Dean named the canon of Goa cathedral as the executor of his estate in Quepém, with the duty of looking after the pious institutions he had founded. This priest's shrewd will was designed to safeguard not only his palace but also those people who had been under his protection. The will has managed to fulfill both wishes, almost to the present day.

---

[74] *Oriente Português, op. cit.*

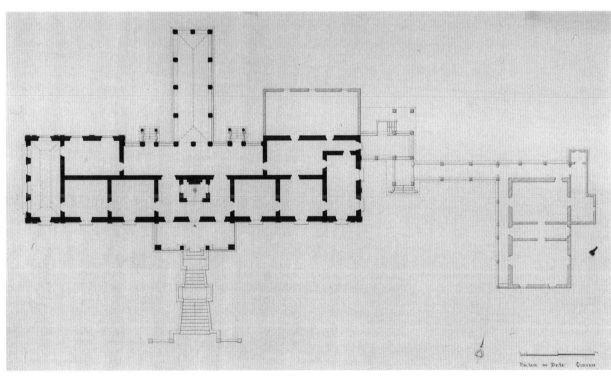

Above and left. *Main façade and plan of the Palácio do Deão in Quepém. Survey by At. H. C.*

Above. *Porched veranda and important architectural complex in the gardens. Palácio do Deão in Quepém*

Lopes Mendes drew a picture of the palace when he was there in 1862. At that time, the building had undergone some alterations which had erased its baroque spirit. Among the new elements was a neoclassical entrance stairway. The old one would have had an S-shape like the two small garden stairs going down to the lake, still visible in 1992. Of the balustrades, vases and stone ornaments, only the sparsest fragments remain. Thanks to Lopes Mendes' sketches, it is possible to reconstitute the design of the entrance pediment, which is today considerably altered.

The few changes made to the interior and on its façade make this building a precious example for the understanding of reciprocal influences between Portuguese and Indian architecture. The structure of the palace, built by a European-born priest, shows an adaptation to

Indian customs. The chapel, placed in the entryway area, brings it close to the concept of a Hindu altar. The similarities with the Santana da Silva palace in Margão, built at the same time, are obvious. In both cases, a long stairway stands immediately facing the chapel, allowing worshipers at the Mass to be seated in a strict order according to their social position.

The rear of the house highlights another aspect linked to the Hindu *vasary*. Starting from a gallery-veranda, another extends perpendicularly, over the garden. Even though the *vasary* form is present in the house, it melts into this much more complex layout which was designed for leisure hours.

As for the design and structure of the façade, there are particularly interesting elements unparalleled in Portuguese architecture. While affirming the Mannerist tradition, the façade is based on a tripartite design with robust Corinthian columns. The entrance porch, which has a narthex form, is balanced on either end by two double pilasters, giving the impression of two distinct structures. In the 18th century, the roofs were probably of the folded design, as old documents attest. In this building, the ends of the façade formed two small turrets crowned by folded roofs like the one at the Santana da Silva palace, built during the same period.

The fact that the entire palace was built on a single, ground floor, contrary to the traditional Portuguese concept of a noble house, is also remarkable. Houses with upper floors reserved for social life had been, since the Middle Ages, synonymous with «manor house», a designation that lasted in Brazil until the end of the 19th century.

Above. *Although greatly altered in relation to its original design, the main entrance still shows features of surprising aesthetic quality. Palácio do Deão in Quepém*

THE SPREAD OF LATE BAROQUE IX

IN THE GREAT HOUSES OF THE BRAHMIN AND CHARDO FAMILIES

The construction of two notable buildings must be highlighted in the second half of the 18th century: the palace of the Santana da Silva family in Margão, and the Bragança palace in Chandor. Both reveal the introduction of the baroque aesthetic in Indo-Portuguese architecture.

This style, which in Goa revealed itself rather as late baroque, was marked by the greater participation of the household in social life. Wealthy families' taste for display and pomp, which up to that time had been restricted to rare social moments such as weddings and christenings while family life was kept highly private, now began to creep more and more into daily life. During the 16th and 17th centuries the chapel had been situated outside and in front of the house, but now it began to be integrated into the house's interior layout. The chapel's presence both added pomp to daily household life and opened the household gradually to the outside. This required a greater intricacy in house layout, with increasingly defined and diversified areas: sitting rooms, drawing room, office, grand reception chamber, and the like.

By the immense size of their houses, their owners expressed the desire to surpass in grandeur the palaces of the Portuguese aristocracy, who during their economic decline became secondary players. The Palácio Bragança results from the joining of two family homes that had belonged to members of the same family. As one entity, they created an importance unequaled in Goa.

Previous page. *Detail of the façade with late Baroque window surrounds. Casa Walfrido Antão in Betalbatim*

117

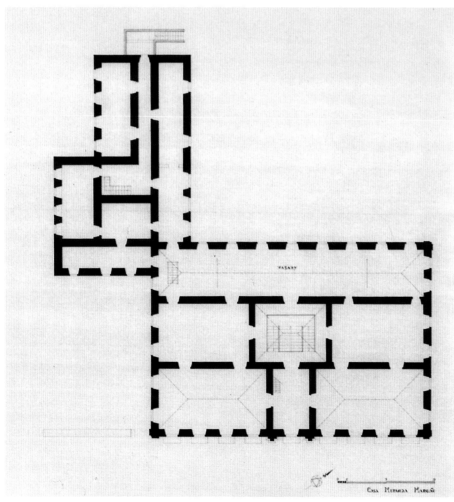

The Santana da Silva house shows more academic planning, with three main façades around a patio. The façades were joined at right angles as in the Carcome Lobo palace in São Pedro. Lopes Mendes' floor plan renderings only show one side façade on the gardens, but the corner with two windows on each side is very obvious. In each palace, a veranda runs along the western-facing lateral façades. During the 18th century, the veranda would have been covered in screens, but in the Santana da Silva palace, glass panes have replaced the screens. The verandas would have provided fresh air and ventilation for the interior rooms opening on to them. The fish-scale pattern of the screens would have provided both protection from rain and free circulation of air.

The veranda was a favoured spot for ladies of the house, as witnessed by Pyrard and other visitors, because they could observe the outside world without being seen themselves.

In the baroque interior layout, the central stairway gained a new, monumental importance, as seen in these two palaces. The stairway split at the first landing into two sym-

metrical sets of stairs, which met again at the first floor in a hall leading into the reception rooms. The staircase thus gave a stage effect to the whole space, which was clearly in accordance with baroque aesthetics. We find the same scheme in grand Portuguese palaces from the mid-18th century, the most refined being the Anadia palace in Mangualde and the Lumiares palace in Lisbon. In Goa, the plan underwent variations of climate and Indo-Portuguese customs.

In the Palácio dos Brangança in Chandor, the stairway is arranged in the form of a porch looking down on a large interior court. The upstairs gallery is made up of three parts, linking the upper landing with the reception rooms facing the façade and the service area situated at the rear. This main distribution centre of the house is in fact a semi-open space with freely circulating air. Plants placed along the stairs and the gallery instill a climate of an interior garden, giving it an exotic and tropical atmosphere. This layout is repeated in the Casa dos Proença in Calangute. The house, which harks back to the 17th century in its

Above and left. *Façade and detail of the entrance to the Casa dos Miranda in Margão*

Previous page. *Main elevation and plan of the main floor of the Casa dos Miranda in Margão. Survey by At. H. C.*

119

Above. *Chapel of the Casa dos Osório Saldanha in Arossim*

Left. *Plan of the main floor of the house. Survey by At. H. C.*

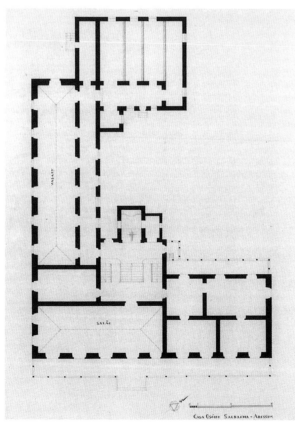

interior layout and façade design, has its staircase in the old central patio, with a similar porch roof. Of smaller proportions, the porch rests on elegant octagonal stone columns with Tuscan capitals. As in the Bragança palace, a semi-open space was most suitable to the hot, humid climate of India.

Returning to the nucleus of staircases in the Santana da Silva palace, we must note that the alteration of its layout was not due to the climate, but to the hierarchy of castes. The chapel was situated on the central landing, while the upper gallery, normally used for reaching the reception rooms, began to function as a tribune for Mass, with people sitting on the three flights of stairs according to their social position.

This model of a staircase with a chapel on the intermediate landing was repeated in the Casa dos Osório Saldanha in Arossim. The chapel there, though somewhat less academic, boasts an interesting group of gilt carvings, including angels showing some Hindu influence. The chapel-staircase relationship observed in the Dean's palace was not only repeated in the homes of native Indian families; the Melo Sampaio palace in Pangim and the Palácio dos Nova Goa in Santa Inês also had their chapels at the midway point on the staircase. Both cases are examples of Hindu cultural influence on the interiors of houses belonging to the Portuguese aristocracy.

While interior staircases provided the dramatic effect that made them baroque features *par excellence*, baroque values were also applied to exterior staircases. With their serpentined, balustraded guard-rails that grew wider near the base, they gave the house's façade a splendid decorative effect.

This design, which would be repeated in the patio house, was closely linked to staircases and entrance steps of churches. The design was found indiscriminately in both civil and religious architecture.

In the patio house, which only had a ground floor, there were fewer opportunities for displaying the dynamic spatial values of baroque architecture. With no staircase needed on the interior, energies were concentrated on the outside of the house, with the result that the steps leading to the front door became highly dramatic. Baroque style could also be practiced on window frames and other decorative details. With the rising social status of the Brahmin families, and their tendencies to one-storey patio houses, the baroque style was used more as a decorative art than as a building scheme.

The baroque tendency for greater decoration of façades became very popular, and this decorative aspect gained greater significance in both patio and two-storey houses. The Mannerist scheme of alternating pilasters and windows was retained, but the pilasters were given new designs, decorated with garlands

Above. *Entrance porch with 18th century curved and counter-curved staircase*

Left. *Balconied window with coiled decoration of religious influence. Casa dos Godinhos in Majorda*

121

Above and right. *Façade and detail of a window from the Casa dos Monteiros in Assolna. Photo H. C.*

and plaster finials, to suit the tastes of the large Goan clientele intent on delighting the senses. Scrolls, garlands and shells also graced window and door frames, many copied from European engravings brought by priests as guides for decorating their new churches in the colony. In the Casa dos Costas in Corturim, the stair banisters are bordered by plaster lanterns, whose *rocaille* design is identical to the sculpted wooden lanterns used in church processions and cortèges.

Because a vast number of churches had been built all over Goa during the 16th and 17th centuries, and because Portugal was now suffering economic decline, fewer churches were built in the baroque period. Besides, carpenters, joiners, plasterers, painters and gilders had more than enough work maintaining and restoring the older churches because of India's erosive climate. These craftsmen also found ample work on civilian projects.

As had been the case during the 16th and 17th centuries, religious architecture still supplied the models and plans for civil architecture, although in this baroque period the influence was limited to interior decoration.

Above and left. *Façade and detail of a window from the Casa Walfrido Antão in Betalbatim. Photo H. C.*

The grandeur that this palace still displays today in Margão clearly shows the power and supremacy that the Brahmin families acquired in the administration of Portugal's empire from the middle of the 18th century. This power had already been conferred on certain families, such as the Frias, Gonçalves and Pereiras, during the 17th century, but it was confirmed and extended in the 18th. This house is a clear testimony to such power.

Construction was begun during the second half of the 18th century under the orders of Ignácio Sebastião Santana da Silva, a personality who for several decades occupied the post of Secretary of State of the Government of the State of India.[75]

The family's permanence in this house and its secure position in the ranks of highest Brahmin nobility transformed the palace into a unique example of Indo-Portuguese architecture and, with its stellar collection of furniture, an archetype for decorative arts.

It remains the only existing palace in Goa with steeply-inclined folded roofs, and the last example of a style which was typical of the grand palaces and Goan convents. It did, however, lose the seven roofs for which it was known in Concanim, *Sat Bunzam'Gor*, and today has only three roofs covering the main building.

The erudite design of the palace implies that an architect was employed to build it, and the natural way in which the palace embodies Goan traditions and Brahmin customs shows

[75] **Abreu**, Miguel Vicente de, *Catálogo dos Secretários de Estado da Índia Portuguesa, desde 1505 até 1866*. New Goa, 1866, pp. 11-12.

Left. *Palácio dos Santana da Silva in Margão. Author's drawing*

Previous page. *Detail of main floor window*

125

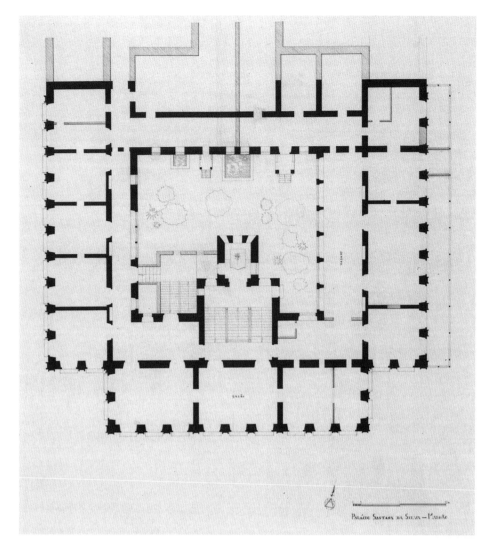

Above. *Plan of the main floor of the Palácio Santana da Silva in Margão. Survey by At. H. C.*

that the architect had a deep knowledge of Goan culture.

The intrinsic linking of the *vasary* to the rest of the interior, the veranda stretching along the entire length of the side of the palace, and the two-storey façade while daily life was carried out on one floor, all these features suggest that the architect was well-versed in contemporary Goan aesthetics and that he was aware of the strictness of Brahmin customs.

While the façade organisation displays careful treatment of the pilaster design, the pediments over the windows reveal a formal and decorative work in the purest Goan tradition of the 17th and 18th centuries. The Mannerist tool of making pilasters stand out in relief and the rhythmic alternance of pilasters and windows are typical Indo-Portuguese features. The balconied main floor windows are also of 17th century design, and it appears that the late baroque style did not give any new twists to these elements.

The central placement of the chapel and its nuclear role in organising interior spaces around it shows that the architect was not only Goan, but that he might have been a priest trained by the Jesuits.

We know from documents[76] that the plans of the city of Mormugão, and most of its construction, were carried out successively by three Jesuit priests. Father Theotónio de Rebello began the works, and was succeeded by Father Ignácio de Almeida, and finally by Father Manuel Carvalho. The successive nomination of three Jesuit priests in the greatest architectural work of the first half of the 18th century proves the importance that the Company of Jesus occupied in architectural planning in Goa. If at the time of the building of this palace, the Jesuits had already been expelled

---

[76] *O Cronista do Tissuary*, New Goa, 1866, p. 280.

Above. *Although characteristic of Indo-Portuguese architecture up to the 19th century, this palace is one of the last examples of a building with folded roof*

Left. *Detail of the main façade's window and pilasters. Palácio Santana da Silva in Margão. Photo H. C.*

from Goa, it would have been natural that they had left behind a school of architects capable of articulating traditional Goan models of great quality.

Revealing a strong grasp of concept and wide experience in religious architecture, the architect placed two windows behind the altar, but at an angle of forty-five degrees, thus creating a subtle lighting effect. Placed in a semi-circular open structure and removed from the wall, the altar is illuminated by imperceptible sources, giving it a rare effect of chiaroscuro.

Situated as the chapel is at the middle landing of the main staircase, the whole gains remarkable grandeur, and retains an ecclesiastic spirit as though it were in a bishop's palace. On climbing the staircase, we cannot but think of the Palácio dos Bispos in Oporto, or other Portuguese examples such as the Palácio dos Condes de Anadia in Mangualde and the Palácio dos Condes de Lumiar in Lisbon. The door frames are crowned by classical pediments with busts, instead of curved baroque pediments, in memory of 17th century Italian Mannerism. The affinities between these and the 16th century windows in the Casa dos Monteiros in Candolim establish a tradition for Brahmin and Chardo families which had been based on palaces of the Portuguese nobility.

The chapel's placement inside the house, however, differs from European standards, where celebrating Mass was a more public activity. In the houses of Portuguese bishops and noblemen, the chapel door and the house door were part of the exterior façade, giving a social function to the chapel which ran counter to Indian sensibilities.

Starting from this central core of chapel and staircase, the rest of the layout developed around a large interior court. Three reception rooms were situated along the main façade,

Left. *Upper landing with access to the reception rooms. The doors, in classic style crowned by pediments and busts, create a link with the windows of the Casa dos Monteiros in Candolim, suggesting a model of reference in the great palaces of the Portuguese nobility*

with a fourth, larger room on the westward façade. This room, which in the 18th century corresponded to an audience chamber, was converted into rooms when the palace was later divided into two residences. Initially the rooms were situated in the coolest part of the palace, along the north façade. The reception room was used for weddings, and is still the traditional *sadery* of Hindu households, due

Previous page. *Central nucleus of stairs with a chapel opening up onto the intermediate landing*

Right. *Detail of the reception room of the palace with a portrait of the builder of the house: Sebastião Inácio Santana da Silva*

130

Right. *The old study with a passage through to the dining room*

Next page. *Forming a long and narrow room, the dining room of the Indo-Portuguese house maintained the features of the vasary of the traditional Hindu house. Palácio dos Santana da Silva, Margão*

to its distance from other areas. Most significant was the dining room, whose proportions and shape preserved the purest spirit of the *vasary*. It opened on to the interior court through a series of screened windows, and acquired an intimacy and a freshness appreciated by Portuguese taste. The veranda on the west wall, where Portuguese influence is most evident, was also screened. Similar to those at the palace of the Counts of Nova Goa and Carcome Lobo, the false, slatted ceiling is decorated with simple motifs. The slats allowed air circulation, cooling the air which had entered through shutters on the lower half of the windows, while the upper halves remained closed.

The huge number of servants in an 18th century household diminished drastically in the 19th century. The service area of this palace was in large part demolished. The interior patio still has a well from which the family drank. Laundry and cooking were carried out with this water, which was kept in a kitchen far removed from that of the servants, to avoid contamination.

The palace would have had pyramid-shaped, slatted wooden ceilings during the 18th century, which have disappeared in subsequent restoration. The staircases and some of the rooms, such as the *vasary*, have kept their original ceilings, whose interesting decorations formed the ventilation grills. The frescoes visible today are no longer of the quality of the originals, but they do evoke 17th century themes and the custom of painting walls to imitate textiles. In the archway of the entrance door and on the chapel walls, there are still frescoes of great quality, imitating woven textiles.

The palace also retains a notable collection of furniture. The number of pieces of furniture in 18th century houses was limited, but here one arm chair stands out among the oldest

Left. *Old wooden divisions, typical of Hindu architecture, in a gallery-veranda. Palácio dos Santana da Silva, Margão*

pieces. It is unlike the other chairs, and would have been the chair from the «throne room» (*sala de estrado*). Two large couches with carved arms were reserved for the ladies of the house. This custom still remains and it is considered bad taste for a man to sit on these couches.

There are also pieces of 19th century furniture throughout the house, and many are influenced by Indian, Portuguese, Chinese and English styles. The English-style chairs are the result of an enormous volume of trade between Goa and England via Bombay. Also of superb quality are some magnificent chandeliers and lamps which were imported from Bavaria via Bombay.

Two 17th century armchairs in the present-day reception room, with the year 1674 carved on their backs, predate the house, and must have come from the Casa do Corturim, where the family had its origins.

Left. *View of the room referred to as «Infante Dom Miguel» in honour of the prince of the House of Braganza's stay at the palace*

Above. *The Bragança Palace in Chandor. Author's drawing*

Following page. *Detail of the main façade of the palace seen from the garden*

The grandeur of its proportions and the complexity of its layout make this palace one of the most interesting examples of all Indo-Portuguese architecture. A careful study of the building reveals construction details which date it to the end of the 18th century.

The palace underwent significant alterations during the 19th century, however, which modified its original design. These make it difficult to clearly identify the features of its design which hark back to the 17th century. It is in the parts of the house face inwards and in the courts that one can see large screened windows and galleries in a style that is earlier than that of the 18th century design seen on the main façade and in the reception rooms. Some of the rooms have ceilings with Hindu-style carved wooden roof trusses, which were used in 17th and 18th century interiors. These lead us to conclude that the building predates the immense 19th century construction.

Apart from the 19th century work, the building also became more complex as a result of the joining of two previously separate residences into a single architectural unit. While there is no available documentation of this event, everything points to the possibility of the ensemble being built in the 18th century as a way of joining the two dwellings. This activity was common in Goa because of a Hindu family tradition that maintained an ever-growing family under the same roof. It was also linked to families' dependency on an agrarian community system where their rights and properties were indivisible. Branches of a family would continue expanding, and would be dependent on the original branch, who in turn had become dependent on the community. This system guaranteed the stability of these families throughout the period of Portuguese domination.[77] The existence of indivisible properties in the hands of single

families explains some of their building structures, which in turn allow us to date these Brahmin and Chardo houses to the arrival of the Portuguese in India.

The Bragança family, constituting the unifying group in this house, is represented by the Bragança Pereiras and the Meneses Braganças. During the 19th century, each one of these families gained importance and each received the title of «Moço Fidalgo» with service in the royal household as well as a coat of arms. These titles were granted to Francisco Xavier de Bragança in 1878 and to António Elzário Sant'Anna Pereira in 1882 under charters issued in Lisbon by the Council of Nobility.[78]

This greater autonomy allowed the palace to become a huge edifice, where one senses a clear attempt, notably in the extension of the façade, to surpass Portuguese noble palaces in luxury and grandeur.

The aesthetic effect of the whole, however, is somewhat monotonous, as there is no tripartite division of the façade or any other effect which would give vibrancy and rhythm to it. The palace seems to have a façade elongated beyond control, while its central section lacks a monumental staircase capable giving the upper floor some balance. The building merely looks a prisoner of its will to overtake its Portuguese rivals. The preoccupation with monumentality does not reach the decorative sophistication that we see in houses of more modest proportion, such as

Above. View of the main façade of the palace with emphasis on the rhythmic alternation of the window-pilaster of mannerist tradition which would remain until the end of the 19th century as a feature of Indo-Portuguese architecture

Right. Central nucleus of stairs in a patio covered by a porch. Photo H. C.

[77] This subject is dealt with in two books by Teotónio de Sousa: *Goa Medieval – A Cidade e o Interior no Séc. XVII*. Editorial Estampa, Lisbon, 1994. Chapters 3 and 4. Organisação e Praxas Agrárias. A Vida Rural, pp. 67-99; and *Rural Economy and Life in Goa Through the Ages*, Goa University, New Delhi, 1990, pp. 78-116.

[78] **Xavier**, Felipe Nery. *Nobiliarchia Goana*. New Goa, I. N., 1862.

those of the Frias and Monteiro families in Candolim, or the Santana da Silva family in Margão.

The reference to Portuguese standards is obvious in the adoption of an upper floor, while houses of Goan families were usually on ground level.

The 19th century transformations were mainly concentrated on building a large ball-room in each residence, but they also affected the façade, as they introduced a style of window fashionable in that period. The decoration of the balconied windows is purely 19th century, with superimposed arches as opposed to straight lintels. The balconies are supported by 18th century corbels; their 19th century counterparts would have had more varied forms. The façade's Tuscan pilasters show 17th century character, as does their alternating with the balconied windows.

Because Goa's cultural environment had become more provincial and more removed from Europe, new aesthetic trends in Europe were introduced here as simple variations from a lexicon of decoration. Local tradition, endowed with a decorative exuberance, con-tinued establishing its own variations on trends arriving from Portugal, but generally held strongly to the Mannerist memories of Italian influence, taking the pilaster-window alte-ration as its own.

The palace retained a salient, 18th century wing, with a windowed gallery identical to those of the Palácio do Deão in Quépem and the Palácio dos Condes de Nova Goa, thereby linking it to the last cycle of great Portuguese houses.

The triangular pediment, flanked by flamboyant stone ornaments and Rococo decoration, accentuated the energy of the façade; an aesthetic value of late Portuguese baroque introduced to Goa in the mid-18th century.

Left. *Central nucleus of the façade crowned by a pediment identical to that of the Palácio dos Condes de Nova Goa in Pangim. Photo H. C.*

Below. *View of the great gallery originally covered by screens, Bragança Palace in Chandor. Photo H. C.*

Analysis of the edifice shows that it had either not been completed in the 18th century, or that the later alterations altered it entirely in the 19th century. The floor plan suggests that the original layout was based on three interior courts, or patios. A central patio would have linked the nucleus of staircases, while two symmetrically located patios would have been built, one for each residence. We can still see a patio forming the basis for the Meneses Bragança side of the palace, but in the current Bragança Pereira dwelling the patio is not closed on all four sides, creating an impression of asymmetry in relation to the central patio.

The floor plan's coherence and symmetry would have been lost during the 19th century alterations, during which, one senses, the two parts of the family wanted to give their living quarters its own identity. Each has a ballroom and gallery, in symmetrical but opposite locations. Given the similarities between this palace and the Palácio dos Condes de Nova Goa, one can suppose that the original façade here might also have had two long verandas. Even though there is today no evidence of such verandas, they would have given the façade a grander, more formal character, similar to that of the Colaço house in Ribandar.

The 19th century transformations to this palace did not entirely eliminate some of the more primitive features which give us data on the floor plan and decoration of the building. The skeleton of the old *vasary* is still perceptible in the Bragança Pereira residence, though it is now divided into two rooms by a wooden panel. Considered to be too long for 19th century European habits, the old chamber was divided in two, with each half now big enough to accommodate a dining room. Running perpendicular to the main façade, the old *vasary* connected the front reception areas to the service areas at the rear of the palace.

Above. *Sequence of arcades facing one of the house's patios.*
Left. *Linking various rooms, the galleries and arcaded verandas served to ventilate the inner rooms during the hot monsoon months. Interior view of the palace's great gallery.*
Photo H. C.

Following pages. *Ballroom decorated in 19th century style.*
Bragança Palace in Chandor

141

Right. View and detail of the old dining room-vasary divided, during the 19th century, as a result of its large size, into two rooms

144

In the residences in both sides of the palace, the rooms are still arranged in the traditional succession of antechamber and audience hall. While audience halls fulfilled the highest social function during the 16th and the 17th centuries, here in the Bragança Pereira house the ballroom continues to perform the same role. An oversized arm chair placed at the center of the rear wall calls the visitor's attention in the same way that a throne would. A series of couches along the side walls are in a Romantic style recalling the audiences given by viceroys. The representation room (*quarto de parada*) is also clearly derived from Portuguese tradition. In the Bragança Pereira apartments it connects directly with the ballroom. It was here that special ceremonies took place, such as the respect and compliments paid on the birth of a child, or when overnight vigils were kept for the recently deceased. Etiquette demanded that during such nights, the family should offer tea and cakes in the room next door to all who came to pay a final tribute to the deceased.

Of particular interest as a remnant of 17th and 18th century Indo-Portuguese traditions was the vast gallery on the Bragança Pereira residence. It had great stone arches running the length of the façade facing the patio. Its shape is reminiscent of descriptions of palaces that have disappeared, such as those of the viceroys and that of the Melo de Sampaio family. Linking a series of reception and other rooms to the exterior, the gallery ventilated the house. The same ventilation function was also fulfilled by the staircase on the central entrance patio. Large pillars form a type of porch in the interior of the patio, creating a vast covered area with freely circulating air. Potted plants on the landings added a garden-like climate to this generously proportioned interior space.

Some of the palace's rooms still maintain their pyramid-shaped ceilings, with their beams carved and gilded in Hindu style, as had

Left. *Gardens of the house seen from the main floor*

been the style of 16th and 17th century palaces such as the Archbishops' Palace in Goa.

Throughout the palace, inlaid flooring of great quality is found, as are the remains of painted wall decoration, helping the visitor to visualise the previous, 18th century interior. Like those in the Santana da Silva palace, the wall paintings reproduce textile patterns, suggesting that in the 17th and 18th century, reception rooms were lined with silk whose vulnerability to the humid climate had led to substituting it with painting.

Both residences in this palace contain a vast collection of furniture, but most of it dates from the late 18th and early 19th century, the period where furniture was introduced in a large-scale way. Chinese influence found its way into furniture shapes in the 18th century, and increased its presence during the subsequent century. Among the 19th century pieces

here is a large arm chair, something found in all the large houses of the day, which must have been a throwback to chairs used for audiences in earlier epochs. Many churches also kept a similar model of such a chair in their sacristies.

What stands out in this vast collection of furniture is Goa's lively capacity for reinterpreting a variety of shapes and designs, giving to Portuguese or Far Eastern models the most liberal variations.

Above and left. *Room used for occasions of pomp and ceremony and late 18ᵗʰ century palanquin. Bragança Palace in Chandor*

IX-3 FROM THE TWO-STOREY CASA DE SOBRADO
TO THE SINGLE-LEVEL CASA DE PÁTIO

Above. Original house of the Noronha in Mandur.

Following page. Detail of the façade with emphasis on the design of the rails with scrolling in Hindu style

As we have already explained, the *casa de sobrado* was difficult to adapt to Hindu living habits, which had always been organised on a single storey arranged around a courtyard. In numerous cases, native families built a house whose façade showed two storeys, but which had only one real floor behind the façade. Taking advantage of sloping land, domestic life could be arranged on a single floor, while a «ground floor» would consist merely of a collection of storage rooms. In the Casa dos Santana da Silva and the Casa dos Gama in Verna, all domestic life took place on one floor, even though their houses appeared to be two-storey buildings. In the Casa dos Miranda in Loutulim, the whole house is arranged around an interior patio, and the lower floor was only an entrance area and a small wing of rooms separated from the daily life of the house.

During the 18th century, as the Brahmin and Chardo families took on more autonomy, the two-storey house lost its importance as the model for a manor house. There were transitional models: houses where the façade shows a low-lying ground floor with small window slits, or shows the lower floor as a kind of remnant of an earlier building – a platform, complete with arches and pilasters that support the «current» main floor.

148

Above. *During the transition from the two floorhouse to the one floor house, the compact effect of the building's basement was diluted by decorations on the arches and pilasters. Casa dos Noronha in Mandur. Photo H. C.*

Right. *Plan of the main floor of the Casa dos Noronha in Mandur. Survey by At. H. C.*

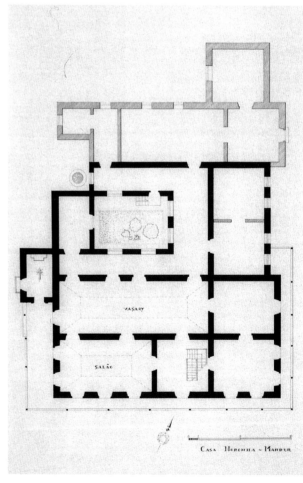

In the Casa dos Noronha in Mandur, the entrance is a low arch at the center of a rather squat arcade designating the lower floor. This lower floor itself forms a platform for the main floor, which is seen as resting on a long porch running the length of the façade.

During the 19th century, this platform was stabilised at a height of a metre and a half, thus allowing a staircase which could access the porch. A wide, covered stairway could give the whole an air of hospitality, without loss of dignity. The platform was integrated into the principal façade, while in the rear, one would descend by various landings to the service areas, their importance marked by their height on the landings.

Above. *Towards the end of the 18th and during the whole of the 19th centuries, the basement in the one floor house was finished off with a sequence of pilasters and small columns. Casa Castelim Aguiar in Varca*

DECORATIVE ARTS AND INTERIOR AESTHETIC CONCEPTS IN THE 18TH CENTURY

The 18th century was marked by the growing secularisation of social life. Religious luxury and ostentation which developed after the Council of Trent and characterised counter-reformation aesthetics during the 17th century were now gradually transmitted to daily life. The house now acquired a representational value in public life which had been previously reserved for the church. As insistence on domestic privacy gave way to greater participation in public life, the house interior changed. Floor plans became more complex, and decoration more permanent. Because the home was opened up to the public so rarely during the 16th and 17th centuries, its owners would mount a decor for the occasion, hanging precious hangings on the wall and getting out the better pieces of furniture and objects. Now, decoration needed a less transient and more permanent nature. There was more pressure to create diversity in furniture and decorative arts, in order to fulfill the different functions for the various reception rooms. The rooms, in turn, became more diversified in their functions.

In Goa, the church's enormous power and Brahmin families' insistence on privacy slowed this evolution, so the changes only took on real significance at the end of the 18th century.

Goa's distance from Portugal, which was now concentrating its efforts on colonising Brazil, left the community to develop interior decoration and decorative arts distinct from those in Portugal. Meanwhile, Chinese exports through Macao, created a taste for *chinoiserie* that was consumed more avidly in Goa than it was in Europe.

Among the rare documents referring to 18th century Goan interiors, an illuminated manuscript from the Deccan school[79] gives us a vivid picture of a refined environment where Portuguese, Indian and Chinese influences intermingled. The lady of the house reclines on a carved and gilded chaise longue of baroque style, the tray and the flower vase in her room suggest Indian brass work. Chinese artwork is revealed in the red lacquered stand under the vase, in the blue and white porcelain, and in the paintings hanging on the wall. But it is the treatment of walls and floor which best define Goan taste of the 18th century. The wall imitates marble, with pilasters dividing it into sections, and displays refined European taste.

Above. *Detail of inlaid flooring. Casa dos Miranda, Loutulim*

Previous page. *Interior of a Goan house shown in an 18th century illumination of the Escola do Decāo. Of inestimable value both socially as well as aesthetically, this interior appears profusely decorated with inlaid work and painting imitating marble*

---

[79] This manuscript, now in a private collection, is reproduced in the work *Islamic Heritage of the Deccan*, Ed. George Mitchell, Marg. Publications, Bombay, 1986, p. 108.

The most exotic aspect of this room is the wainscoting on the walls, which became very popular in Goa during this period. It must have originated in the 18th century, when this decorative pebbled technique was used in fountains and garden ornaments. The garden benches at the Bragança palace are decorated this way. The availability of large quantities of porcelain and cheap labour in Goa, even during periods of crisis, favoured the development of this technique, which was soon applied to interiors. The application on walls, however, must have been more unusual, as it was normally applied in open air loggias.

In surviving 18th century interiors, what stands out today are the frescoes imitating textiles, in reference to the previous custom of decorating churches and reception rooms with silk and damask. Kloguen referred to this custom during the early 19th century when he wrote: «*the parish churches in the diocese are built nearly on the same plan. On solemn occasions, all the walls of the church are hung up and covered with rich silk stuffs.*»

In the baroque period, decoration became more permanent, and ornaments heretofore portable became fixed elements in an interior. But the humid climate prevented people from using real cloths on the wall. The main living

Above and right. *Detail of the reception room and back of a chair. Santana da Silva Palace, Margão*

room in the Santana da Silva palace is still «covered» with an imitation of damask that has great effect. While the painting in the house is no longer the original 18th century work, the frescoes in the chapel imitating cloth hangings – one over the entrance arch and one on the inside walls – are the original paintings.

Other painted patterns imitating cloth may be found in reception rooms in the Santana da Silva and Bragança palaces. They are, however, in a very poor state of repair, due to 19th century alteration work in both houses.

The pebbled masonry work decoration of the floors may be seen in various rooms and corridors in the Bragança palace. The variety of patterns shows the Indian penchant for strong colouring. Because this technique is more resistant than the wall painting, there remain many surviving examples in both Salcete and Bardez provinces. In the Casa dos Miranda in Loutulim, the Casa dos Assis in Colva and the Casa dos Abranches in Verna are all 18th century houses in which this technique was applied with remarkable creativity. On one floor in the Abranches house, the technique was applied alternately with ceramic tiles in a checquer-board pattern. It suggests that the floor might have previously been tiled, as were

Above and left. *Detail of two floors showing inlaid work.
Casa Assis Fernandes in Verna*

155

period in which furniture was introduced for daily use. The virtual non-existence of beds is due to the use of *esquifes*, a type of simple bed frame on turned feet with interlaced canvas for support. This type of bed was better adapted to Goa's hot, humid climate. Bedframes hanging from the beams were also used until the 18ᵗʰ century. In the Casa dos Piedade Costa in Majorda, one can see some enormous pieces of wood hanging from the ceiling beams. The strength of these pieces attests to their use as beds. In the 19ᵗʰ century, metal hoops were more frequently used, but they were less resistant and would have been used for babies' cots.

The inlaid furniture made in Goa during the 17ᵗʰ century which lent such grandeur to Portuguese palaces was so rare in Indo-Portuguese houses that one may assume these pieces were made mostly for export, and used exclusively in Goa by Portuguese families. Production for the Goan market was primarily in carved furniture. Indian artisans built remarkable sculpted furniture, carved into veritable lace forms, using the most rare and precious of exotic woods.

Unlike the Indians, the Chinese demanded more furniture from the Ming period on, and showed a refined aesthetic sense in the design of their pieces. Goa's expanding trade links with Macao brought a greater dissemination of Chinese furniture designs during the 18ᵗʰ century. Typical Chinese decorative features in 18ᵗʰ century chairs show the great influence of the Chinese culture.

As in the previous century, furniture was scarce in Goan houses in the 18ᵗʰ century. The same furniture shapes appeared in nearly all the houses of native families. Among these were a heavily decorated chair referred to as a corner chair, a couch with an inclined backrest and a set of four chairs. Armoires or cupboards were virtually non-existent. In the *vasary* as in the bedrooms, possession were arranged on

the Church of São Caetano in Goa and the first Pinto palace in Candolim.

As for furniture in great Goan houses, there is a real lack of early 18ᵗʰ century pieces, and an even greater paucity of 17ᵗʰ century pieces. For Indian families, furniture had little importance and was limited to small objects of daily use: trays, small boxes and chests. A family's wealth was concentrated in jewels or in textiles woven with silver and gold.

Older furniture in most Goan palaces is limited to two types of arm chairs and a deep-seated couch from the early 18ᵗʰ century, the

Reception room with furniture of European and Chinese influence. Bragança Palace, Chandor

shelves in niches in the walls. In the most important rooms, doors had carved and sculpted panels, often in a radiating pattern. This pattern was also used in 17th century religious buildings, particularly in convents.

The existence of only one large armchair in a household suggests that it was designed to maintain a 16th century Portuguese tradition of reserving a large chair for the owner of the house. The chair, closely linked to the concept of a throne, was used by the church during the whole of the 19th century. This throne-chair type, of which there are many examples, was first studied by Maria Helena Mendes Pinto.[80]

The couches, which we find in old Goan families, had a very private use. They were reserved for the mistress of the house and the female members of her entourage. The depth of the seat was determined by the habit, until the 18th century, of ladies sitting with their legs crossed, a custom which also remained in Portugal. In the same spirit, some residential chapels have a very low gilded wooden bench, in the form of an ottoman, whose delicate decoration indicates that it was reserved for the lady of the house.

As a whole, Goan furniture shows itself to be an adaptation of a Lusitanian architectural model, where decoration becomes preponderant. With a ceaselessly renovated creativity, Hindu and Chinese motifs treat European themes, in which these diverse influences are liberally interpreted.

Above. *Ladies' stool from the end of the 18th century. Carried by a slave, these stools always accompanied the ladies of the upper classes whenever they visited churches*

---

[80] **Pinto**, Maria Helena Mendes, in *Oceanus, «Sentando-se em Goa»* (Sitting in Goa). N.[rs] 19, 20. Sept.-Dec., 1994. pp. 43-58.

THE CASA DE PÁTIO MODEL X

AND THE CONFIRMATION OF LOCAL FEATURES IN INDO-PORTUGUESE CIVIL ARCHITECTURE

The patio house was undoubtedly the model best adapted to Indian living standards, and it would serve throughout the latter half of the 18th century and all of the subsequent century as the standard for the Indo-Portuguese house.

The large number of these houses throughout Goan territory shows an emphasis on this type of architecture which was not only appropriate for the climactic conditions and surrounding landscape, but which revealed profound cultural roots.

Beyond the identical nature of these houses' formal structure, this architecture provides an intrinsic aesthetic unity enriched by continually changing ornamental details.

By calling on highly-refined craft traditions in joinery and stucco-work, the porches, staircases, columns, veranda rails and eaves in these houses took on new forms through which the Indian feeling for colour, particularly strong hues, could add ever-new notes of exoticism.

Many of the native tendencies and characteristics which had developed timidly during the 18th century now took on a bolder, more permanent nature. For instance, the central patio, which in the 18th century was typically but not always enclosed, was closed up entirely in the 19th century, becoming a central and controlling element for the layout of the building.

While this patio never took on the shape of the traditional Hindu *raj angan*, it does approach the traditional form in some houses such as those of the Miranda family in Revorá

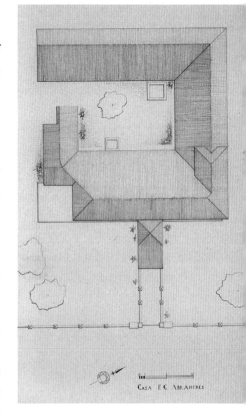

Above. *Plan showing location of the Casa Abranches in Verna. Survey by At. H. C.*

Previous page. *Interior patio of the Casa dos Miranda in Revorá*

161

or the Loyola family. One of its features was a colonnaded gallery surrounding it. In the Casa dos Mirandas in Revorá, the columns have their base in a low wall, which forms a sort of bench all the way around the patio.

With regard to the façade design, as mentioned earlier, the patio house had a tripartite floor plan consisting of two wings stretching out laterally from a main central entrance. The primary façade assumed the dominant position over the side walls, which were only functional walls serving to link the house to the service areas. All decorative efforts were concentrated on the main façade, and here the ancient tradition of stucco work gave full vent to the builder's imagination. The late baroque decorative style took hold in Goa, and was heightened as Indian exoticism crept in alongside it. Partly out of climactic necessity, and partly due to the gradual opening up of the family to social participation, the screened verandas typically found on the side wings began to wind their way around the front façade, also.

Gradually, the veranda took the form of a long porch with a roof, stretching across the façade as long balcony, but still divided by partitions. The Alemão family house in Betalbatim and the Godinho Vaz house in Majorda are good 18th century examples.

Near the end of the century, the veranda became more important as it became the favourite spot for sitting during leisure hours. The family's concern for privacy had fallen away, screens were no longer necessary, and decorative energies were now concentrated on the veranda railings and the wooden columns supporting the eaves over the veranda. In some very elaborate cases, the columns were sculpted and gilded. In the Bragança Pereira house in Utorda, the columns are decorated with grooves and Corinthian capitals. Although this is not the only example, it is the most exqui-

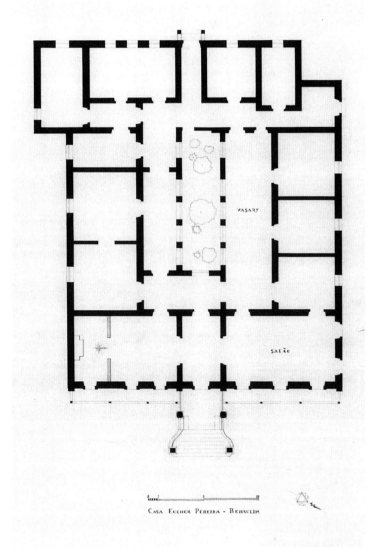

CASA EUCHER PEREIRA - BENAULIM

site. In other houses, such as that of the Monteiros in Assolna, the influence of altar columns is evident, underlining the persistent influence in Goa of religious forms in domestic architecture.

During the 19th century, decorative forms became less dependent on ecclesiastical shapes, and even somewhat less reliant on Portuguese influences of the late baroque. Veranda rails, columns and eaves took on exotic shapes, with finials and rosettes. But constant attacks from the climate reduced their numbers every year. Indented eaves have become harder to find.

Above and left. *Details of the wood work of doors and protection area of the Casa dos Eucher Pereira in Benaulim. Photo H. C.*

Previous page. *View of the façade and plan of the Casa dos Eucher Pereira in Benaulim. Drawing and survey by At. H. C.*

163

Window shutters and fan lights also became more elaborate in their design, with Hindu decorative patterns given free reign.

The supports for these veranda balconies remained, as they had been during the 17ᵗʰ and 18ᵗʰ centuries, composed of three small corbels – proof of the slow evolution and deep conservatism in architectural design in Goa.

The veranda eaves progressively melted into the main roofline, so that the principal roof extended out over the balcony, supported by thick columns. In the Casa dos Cabrais in Nagoa, the columns are decorated with leaves in stucco relief inspired by columns at church altars.

Over all these surfaces, carpenters and craftsmen freely expressed themselves, giving vent to their exuberant imagination, with varied designs and bright colours, giving these buildings an unmistakably Indian touch. But the most characteristic element of the patio house was no doubt the entrance porch, where most of the decorative energies were concentrated, and whose structural evolution reveals to us the evolution in taste of Goans of the late 18ᵗʰ and 19ᵗʰ centuries.

Previous page and above. *Main façade and detail of the veranda forming a half moon in front of the entrance to the chapel. Casa Bragança Pereira in Utorda. Photo H. C.*

X-1 THE BALCONY AND THE ENDURANCE
OF INDIAN TRADITION
IN THE INDO-PORTUGUESE HOUSE

Above. *Typical house with central porch in Verna. Drawing by the author*

Following page. *Porch covered in screens. Casa Filipe Abranches in Verna. Photo H. C.*

The entrance porch is of particular interest in the evolution of Indo-Portuguese architecture, because while its origin was Portuguese, it assumed special significance in the Goan house.

Documents show that the viceroy's and archbishop's palaces in Goa city were endowed with wide staircases culminating in porches. Until the 19th century, the fortress palace of the viceroys had a porch with large Tuscan columns and two flights of stairs with landings. The archbishop's palace, next to the cathedral, had two porches that were entrances to the main floor; one linking the chapel to the palace and the other reaching the audience hall's ante-chamber. These 16th and 17th century porches performed a social function within the sumptuous and scenic rituals developed by the Portuguese in India.

Domestic privacy, pertaining primarily to women, restricted the use of porches for recreational purposes. Leisure moments were spent in the gardens, which were protected by high walls and hidden from the street, while allowing the ladies to look out through screened verandas. The progressive secularisation of domestic life around the mid-18th century allowed for the opening up of houses and the involvement of women in social life. But this change in social mores was only adapted in a very limited way by Brahmin and Chardo families, who were still forbidden from contact with lower castes.

When Portuguese families received a visitor, the person entered the house through what had formerly been the ante-chamber. Linschoten described the custom at the end of the 16th century: «*When any common man goeth to visite an other in his house...and so leadeth him up into his hall or chamber...where he offereth a chaire to sit downe, and then hee himselfe sitteth by him....*»[81]

In Brahmin and Chardo houses, members of lower classes were not allowed to enter, as their presence was felt to defile the living space. The distance from the house that a lower caste member was required to stay was in proportion to the level of his caste; an untouchable would not be allowed even to pass through the gateway into the patio or courtyard.

The porch of the Indo-Portuguese house resolved this problem perfectly, as it created a room outside the house which was treated as a protective ante-chamber to the interior. The

---

[81] **Linschoten**, *op. cit.*, vol. I, p. 195.

Left. *Evolving over various centuries, the Indo-Portuguese house displayed a notable coherency and a capacity to interpret influences, adapting itself to its own style and form. Casa dos Rebelo in Anjuna*

169

porch also satisfied feminine curiosity about passers-by or people approaching the house, because although it was outside, it was now used for domestic life. The porch therefore assumed a fundamental role in both the façade design and, by virtue of its function as an entrance hall, the interior layout.

Although they became common only towards the end of the 18th century, porches had appeared in early forms on 17th century patio houses. Their supporting columns had been of stone, in Tuscan style imitating those of Portuguese noblemen's palaces. Early columns appeared as pillars, resembling those found at old convents, the side entrances of churches, and 17th century ecclesiastical schools. During the 19th century, exuberant tastes required that the pillars become columns, and as they did they became increasingly elaborate: they began to sprout floral motifs, approaching in style the columns at old Hindu temples.

As a leisure area, the porch acquired great symbolic value in 19th century patio houses. Numerous formal and decorative variations reflected the family's prestige. The steep, folded roofs which had characterised the houses of Portuguese nobility for several centuries, now took their final step as markers of aristocracy. Meanwhile, they retained their ventilating function with overhead grills which allowed hot air to escape.

As a variation on a room capable of receiving outside guests, the porch appears to be linked to the practice of the *mandó* and other traditional dances. Developed mainly by the Brahmins, but practiced also by Chardo families, these dances had a privileged stage setting during evening performances on the porch.[82] Porches were equipped with long

[82] **Sardo**, Susana. «Goa Sons e Silêncios». In *Oceanos*, N.ᵒˢ 19-20, 1994, p. 250.

Above and left. *Entrance porch and detail of the main façade of the Casa dos Assis Fernandes in Colva.*
Photo H. C.

Previous page. *Porch of the Casa Estonando de Sá in Siolim.*
Photo H. C.

171

stone benches, and small seats were placed on the steps for servants.

On the side ends of the porch, windows were added for better viewing purposes and for protection from rain. With the introduction of glass, the windows could be larger. Indian taste was revealed here, too, with the use of coloured glass to create a special luminosity and an exotic atmosphere.

Because the porch was so visible and so important to daily life, it was often endowed with highly worked screens, and the best examples of screenwork has come from porches. Fan-lights were also objects of great crafts-

manship; houses are still found with fan-lights imitating peacock's tails, in clear Hindu inspiration.

While the porch was introduced to Goa by the Portuguese, it ended up by playing a significant role in making the native Indian household more sociable. The *mandó* and other musical activities acquired in it their own special place, and, as an architectural feature capable of generating new contacts between castes, the porch spread a humanist influence over Goa that had Christian roots.

Above. *Interior of the porch emphasizing its feature of leisure area adapted to the great monsoon heats. Catholic family house in Corturim*

COLONIAL «POMBALISM» IN NEW GOA
AND 19TH CENTURY
NEO-CLASSICISM

We have seen how, during the dissemination in Goa of the late baroque style, this stylistic tendency was integrated into previous architectural norms as a decorative standard. Neo-classicism, on the other hand, was virtually ignored. In most of the cases where neo-classicism did leave a trace, it was only in the form of minor decorative details, and they never acquired the status of a local fashion. The late baroque and Rococo styles adapted themselves far more easily to the decorative tastes of the Indian population, and to the aesthetic traditions planted here by the Portuguese during the 16th and 17th centuries.

The construction of Pangim as the new Portuguese capital in the region had almost no repercussions at all on civil architecture practiced by local populations. The center of the new colonial city presents, even today, a model of official, administrative architecture, in contrast to the Bairro das Fontainhas (Fontainhas quarter), a neighbourhood which reveals a much more organic concept of urban design. Financial difficulties in the empire and Lisbon's shift of attention towards Brazil caused significant delays on the projects of Viceroy Dom José Pedro da Câmara, who, between 1774 and 1779, made enormous efforts to build a new capital at Pangim, or, at the very least, renovate the existing capital in Goa city. The Pangim initiative was part of an overall strategy of the Marquess of Pombal, who envisioned a new form of centralising political power and a new urban and architectural style to represent it. The work, however, was not carried out during Pombal's time,

Previous page. View of Pangim and the Largo da Câmara at the end of the 19th century. It is still possible to see the rational aesthetics of the New Goa urban project which today is totally unrecognisable. Paul and De Sousa Archives, Pangim

Below. Square in front of the old Palácio dos Vice-Reis in Pangim

175

Above. *Late-Pombaline architectural complex in Pangim. Photograph from the end of the 19th century. Paul and De Sousa Archives, Pangim*

but was begun during the reign of Viceroy Dom Manuel de Portugal e Castro (1827-35). His reign was mainly responsible for the urban definition of the new city and the construction of the architectural complex of the Praça do Município (municipal plaza) and the barracks for the Artillery, Municipal Guard and Reserve regiments. The project strayed significantly from the original proposal, but did preserve a uniform aspect, and a monumental plan in relation to the Mandovi River. Between 1835 and 1844, a series of military rebellions and palace coups, together with the formation of the provisional Privy Council Committees, delayed work again, but it resumed under the more stable regimes of José Ferreira Pestana and the Count of Torres Novas.

Although built at a rather late date, but still within the aesthetic guidelines of the Pombal regime in Lisbon, the new city's architecture was an affirmation of authority, diluted only by the distance and oceans separating it from the kingdom's center. The grid arrangement of streets and the symmetry so esteemed by Lisbon's school of urban planning instilled a rationalism in Pangim's center. The proportions of the two-storey buildings, however, gave it an atmosphere of agreeable colonial provincialism. The uniformity of the architecture offered no polarising features that would have provided a visual impact suitable to the philosophy of exerting authority that was so cherished in Lisbon. The new capital lacked the large plazas with arcades that could be found in Lisbon's Terreiro do Paço, and it also lacked monuments and triumphal arches. The only landmark, the Torre da Câmara (City Council tower) collapsed and was demolished. The result was that the town square lost its geometric focus and the symbol necessary to represent the city as a capital.

Above. *Bairro da Fontainhas area, next to the Conde de Linhares bridge. Photograph from the end of the 19th century. Paul and De Sousa Archives, Pangim*

Under the strict urban planning program, the new palaces of the nobility and wealthy merchants did not stand out from the uniform architectural complex. The palaces of the Counts of Mahém, the Viscounts of Dempó, and the Gama Pinto family were among these. On top of that, alterations undertaken during this century have destroyed the unity and coherence of the urban complex. As a result, we are once again obliged to rely on old documents and the valuable photographs taken during the 19th century by Paul and De Sousa.

State policy, denoted by an emphasis on functionality, stripped façades of their pilasters and eaves, removed the corbels from balconies and the decorations from window frames. All these changes broke away drastically from the styles that had taken root over three centuries. In addition to being aesthetically incompatible with local taste, the policy had also lost the inspired absolutism applied by Pombal to his plans to rebuild Lisbon and the cities in Brazil. Although the Pombaline programme foresaw razing the old Mamais palace, which occupied the land next to the government palace, the demolition was never carried out, and the palace survives today.

As previously stated, Portugal's political and economic instability during the 19th century reinforced the autonomy and power of the privileged classes in Goa. In contrast to Portugal, where a new aristocracy emerged from the liberal wars, in India the old families survived, thrived, and gained increasingly prominent roles in both administrative and economic domains.

That helps to explain the insignificant impact which Pombaline aesthetics had on Indo-Portuguese architecture. The Mannerist

177

and baroque styles were far more suited for what was a romantic eclecticism in 19th century Goa. While the patio house model spread, the large old houses belonging to Goan aristocracy were also restored. In asserting their cultural values and lifestyle, Goa's upper classes integrated the Mannerist and baroque styles in their traditional dwelling models, creating a profoundly original architectural heritage.

In the domain of official architecture, 18th century neo-classicism did make a slight, but late, impact. We find examples of its pronounced decorative style, imitating rustic and cleaved stonework, in the houses of the Rebelo and Mascarenhas families in Anjuna and the Almeida family house in Benaulim. Only in the Almeida house does the style take on a certain unity: here there is no veranda on the façade, leaving in full view the windows which

are framed in imitation rustic stone work, and the corners in cracked stone.

An exceptional example is the Casa dos Roldão de Sousa in Velsao. Unparalleled in Indo-Portuguese civil architecture, a neo-Palladian classicism is exuded from the porch pediment and columns. The cause for such a digression from local style is simple: this family of rich merchants had emigrated to Zanzibar during the 19th century, and the porch style came from that English colony. Remarkably, this influence did not spread through the rest of the building.

In conclusion, the Pombaline style had no repercussions on Indo-Portuguese houses, as neo-classicism was a late-comer to Goa, and itself was already imbued with the eclecticism of the late 19th century and of our own century.

Above. *As an exception to the rule, the Casa dos Almeidas in Benaulim shows neo-Classic style influences based on late-Pombaline origins although integrated in a traditional Indo-Portuguese civil architectural structure. Photo H. C.*

Previous page. *Neo-Classic porch of English influence in the Casa dos Roldão de Sousa in Velsao. This influence is explained by this families' emigration to Zanzibar in the 19th century*

Although the patio house style became somewhat standardised as it became the favoured model for Catholic Brahmin and Chardo families during the second half of the 18th century and the 19th century, it did display some variations both in interior layout and external appearance.

The increasing importance of porch and verandas, which extended the length of the main façade, transferred decorative emphasis away from window frame and towards verandas. In the transformation of porch into veranda, we find stylistic variations. The houses of the Eucher Pereira family in Benolim, the Cabrais in Nagoa, and the Quadros Costa in Loutulim all show these. While the fashion for verandas caused these houses to lose the porch, which had been an important feature in the symbolic and living layout of the

Indo-Portuguese house, it did solve a major construction problem. The creation of a long, deep roof which could stretch down over the veranda formed a useful shield from monsoon rains which had previously infiltrated houses. It is not by chance, then, that these three houses, which have preserved some of the most valuable interiors and carved ceilings of Indo-Portuguese architecture, all have such roofs.

In its interior spaces, the floor plan of the patio house model established, with a fairly repetitive scheme and few variations, a fairly standard form. There was therefore a balance between the representational values of the façade and porch, and the domestic habits practiced inside by the Christianised Goan castes.

The concept of a house on several floors, whose design related the interior and exterior

Previous page. *Interior patio of the Casa dos Fernandes in Chandor*

Below. *Main façade of the Casa dos Cabrais in Nagoa. Photo H. C.*

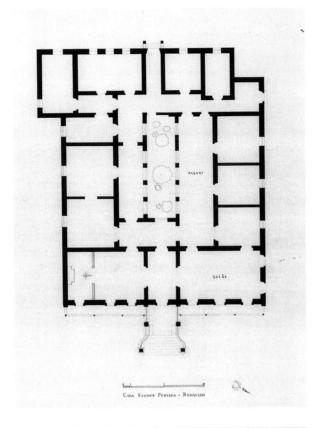

CASA EUCHER PEREIRA - BENAULIM

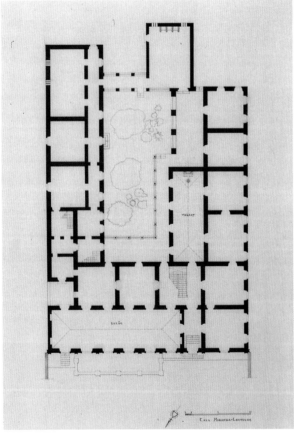

CASA MIRANDA-LOUTULIM

layouts, was unknown in Hindu tradition. But it was integrated in the patio house model, and reinterpreted by the natives, who added to it their own practices.

The balcony and reception rooms had a rapport with the outside, but domestic life remained primarily directed inward, towards the central patio. Acting as a central force for the interior layout, it generated a set of surrounding spaces which were independent from the façade and porch. The façade remained an autonomous body with representative functions. A narrow corridor linked the porch to the dining room – the old Hindu *vasary* – but at the end of the corridor was a second door, which was usually kept closed. It led the way to the house's private areas, to which access was much more controlled. Unlike European or Portuguese houses, where a porch was merely a transition to an entrance hall, this corridor in the Indo-Portuguese house – which is found in all great houses – had a restrictive function, protecting the house's private core.

Running at right angles to the façade, the corridor also established a distribution axis for the rest of the interior layout. The only significant variation of this layout was the location of the dining room, which, as the principal sacred area of the Hindu house, remained the principal structural feature of the family's daily life.

Because of its length, the *vasary* established the link between the family's living rooms and the service area. Normally, the *vasary* would be parallel to the façade, joined at its center with the entrance corridor. Sometimes it would be placed to the rear of the patio, but still parallel to the façade. This more traditional setting ensured greater privacy to the sacred part of the house, emphasised at times by placing a veranda over the central patio, which itself was connected to the entrance corridor. This layout was typically found in more complex, grandiose houses. In the Loyóla Furtado house in Orlim, this layout meant two interior patios, which broke down interior spaces and gave views within the interior, giving the house a refined and palatial air.

In a third variation, the *vasary* was situated perpendicularly to the façade. According to the oldest Vedaic tradition, this was the purest place for it to be. Examples are found in old Brahmin palaces, such as the Mamais palace in Pangim. At the end of this room was the altar to the house's ancestors. The Miranda and the Figueiredos families in Loutulim, two Brahmin families of the highest lineage in Goa, followed this format for their palaces. The Figueiredos house has lost its original structure due to massive alterations at the end of the last century, when it was given a new side wing with a second porch.

This new wing gave the house a palatial dignity by spreading out in an extremely long, single-storey façade. It was surrounded by palm trees and had a view over a magnificent valley.

Reception rooms, usually near the main façade, were often divided by porch and corridor, creating a wing with one large reception room on one side, and a group of smaller reception rooms in the opposing wing. On special occasions, such as weddings, these rooms could be connected by opening a series of large doors. The sacred character of these moments required an intimate relationship with the house's chapel, and the chapel therefore tended to open directly on to the reception rooms. This proximity of chapel and salons was unknown in Portugal. During the 18th century, when the chapel acquired a stronger presence in both urban and country villas, it was built so that it could function independently from the house's inner rooms, and had a door opening directly on to the street. The great chapel of the Loyóla Furtado

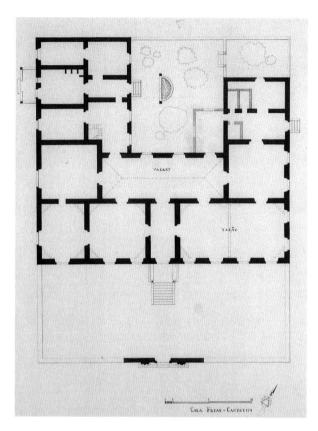

Left and below. *Plans of the Casa dos Costa Frias in Candolim and of the Casa dos Loyóla Furtado in Orlim. Survey by At. H. C.*

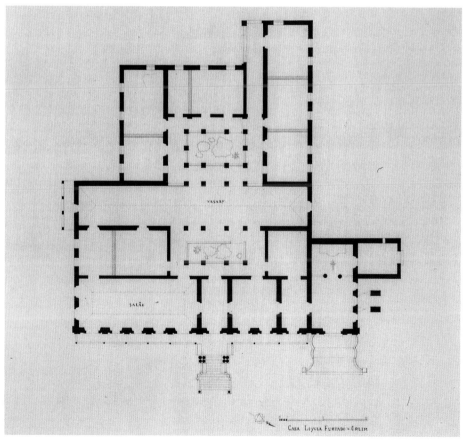

Above. *Façade giving onto the gardens of the Casa dos Roldão de Sousa in Velsao.*
Photo H. C.

in Orlim had a street door, but it retained the door on the house side in order to comply with old family customs.

The unchanging character of patio house floor plans reveals the endurance of local customs, which were kept alive for centuries. It also underlined the fact that Brahmin and Chardo families maintained longstanding privileges throughout the Portuguese colonial period.

INTERIORS AND THE ROMANTIC ATMOSPHERE X-4
OF THE INDO-PORTUGUESE HOUSE

With the exception of some great palaces built during the second half of the 18th century, it was the end of the century and the passage of the 19th century that saw Goan families develop the exuberant luxury which made them famous. Their wealth was closely linked to commerce which Goa established with China, Africa and Brazil, most notably the opium trade. Although episodic, this trade renewed Goa's economy and the health of the family fleets of Goan shipowners.

An endless number of objects of the most diverse origins, from English furniture and Bavarian chandeliers to Chinese porcelain, gives evidence of commerce embracing several continents, in which Portugal did not play an important role.

The Portuguese colonists' tradition of providing higher education to the sons of Brahmin and Chardo families was not lost on the native families. While the Portuguese aristocracy displayed a vocation for military carreers, Goans of noble birth were more concerned that their sons receive a liberal education at the hands of the Jesuit priests.

In 1844, a medical school was officially founded in Goa, and courses were given at the royal hospital. Documents show that courses had already been given there since the end of the 17th century, as Brahmins were referred to as being «university professors» and «physicians general»[83], posts which were conferred by royal decree. These medical studies formed doctors who eventually spread out over the whole of the Portuguese empire during the first half of the 20th century.

For other studies, students could attend not only Lisbon University, but the universities of Bombay and London. Magazines and literature in general during the whole of the 19th century were of a particularly high standard, and Goa's upper castes formed an intellectual elite unequaled among their social peers throughout India.

The study or library became just as vital a part of a house interior as were the reception

Below. *Detail of the interior, open onto the central patio in the Casa dos Fernandes in Chandor*

---

[83] **Saldanha**, Padre M. J. Gabriel de, *op. cit.*, vol. II, p. 296.

rooms used for pompous occasions. While the 17th or 18th century study would have been situated in a wing independent from the social areas, it began now to appear as one or two rooms following on from the reception rooms. They would be used for visits, or receiving guests on special occasions.

Some of the reception rooms contained a gallery at one end where musicians could play. The custom for parties and dinners to be accompanied by a small orchestra was an old one, recorded by foreign visitors as early as the end of the 16th century. The musicians' gallery was usually located above the entrance. Here a door gave access to a mezzanine floor where there was a balcony overlooking the ballroom, whose ceiling height was even greater than that of the entrance hall. Such a balcony may be seen in the houses of the Loyola Furtados in Orlim and the Mascarenhas in Anjuna.

As interiors were used more frequently for socialising, decorative details became even more important than they had been when first introduced during the 18th century. Wall painting imitating textiles, intricately carved ceilings, floors inlaid with small stones now grew in variety of design. Because many 18th century houses were restored in the 19th century, it is sometimes difficult to date these decorative features.

Above. *Detail of the interior decoration of the ballroom of the Bragança Palace in Chandor*

Right. *Detail of the inlay work of the floor. Reception room in the Casa dos Assis Fernandes in Colva. Photo H. C.*

Following page. *View of the interior of the Casa Roldão de Sousa in Velsao and detail of Romantic decoration*

The quality and skill of joiners was displayed in full glory in the carved wooden ceilings. The ceilings' functional roles as ventilating tools ensured their significance, and therefore the need to decorate them. Their use in church ceilings also meant that a school for joiners had been created, and assured a quantity of commissions and diversity of locations that in turn gave rise to much experimentation in the craft. Countless rose and rosette designs are reminiscent of the Portuguese *alfarge* technique of Arab geometric origin. The Casa dos Vinte e Quatro in Goa followed Lisbon rules directly in this regard. Until quite recently, it formed part of the master carpenter's examination, during which he would be required to carve *zimbros,* stars and *rosas* floral pieces.

Goan furniture also diversified during the 19th century, prolonging the movement begun the century before. European and Chinese forms for chairs, sideboards, cupboards, tables and beds were borrowed by Goan artisans, who then added specifically Goan decorative elements, creating a unique furniture style.

It was perhaps the chair with hinged armrests which, as a result of its omnipresence in Goan houses and its exotic role, acquired the highest significance in Goan interior furnishings. First introduced by the Portuguese

Left. *Two details of interior Romantic decoration. Casa dos Monteiros in Assolna and Bragança Palace in Chandor*

who had brought it from China, the chair used for relaxing in evokes visions of hours spent in the shade of a veranda. Thanks to its hinges, the chairs were easily moved around to seat varying groups of people, and were brought inside at night.

In addition to the hinged chair, one or two couches became part of the required furniture in sitting rooms. Placed in a prominent position, the couch was the privileged place for ladies in Indian etiquette, which dictated a strict, hierarchical order for all present.

Previous page. *The division of the window shutters into two separte units allowed for the cooling of the air in the rooms through the openings in the lower part of the shutters. Casa dos Eucher Pereira in Benaulim*

189

X-5   THE CASA LOYÓLA FURTADO IN ORLIM

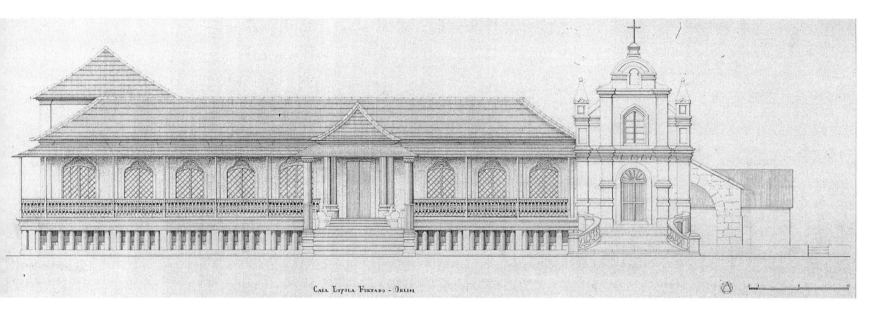

Casa Loyóla Furtado - Orlim

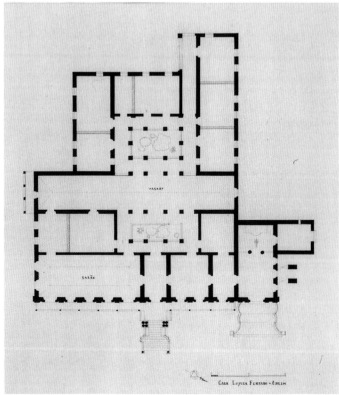

Casa Loyóla Furtado - Orlim

The house's last owner, Doctor Álvaro Loyóla Furtado, left his family estate to a religious institution, and this great house is today a school for children.

Its interior layout has suffered no alterations, and the complexity of its floor plan and façade design make it one of the most remarkable examples of Indo-Portuguese houses. Differing from the Indo-Portuguese tradition, the chapel is not placed within the house; nor is it situated in a courtyard as would be the case in Portuguese family houses. Rather, it is placed next to the house, its façade is contiguous with that of the house façade, though in a clearly distinctive, religious style and with its own stairway.

While Portuguese tradition ruled the 17th century, and chapels remained outside the manor house, Indian tradition prevailed in the 18th century, and chapels were integrated in the house floor plans. But here the chapel appears to function independently from the house, and the device of linking house and chapel façades goes back to the 16th century, evoking the design of many of the churches in Salcete.

It is in the chapel's relation to the house's reception rooms that the Indian nature of this chapel is revealed. While the chapel in a Portuguese noble's house would be integrated in community life rather than household life, Indian caste laws restricted its use to family ceremonies or small groups, quite apart from the community at large.

The façade of this house also makes it one of the best examples of the patio house style, and of 19th century Indo-Portuguese civil architecture. The central porch with its hip roof, large columns and wide staircase commanded attention and decorative energies. Benches placed on the porch that runs the length of the façade remind us of the role the porch fulfilled in daily life. Placed on mid-and

lower levels of the staircase were benches for servants and members of lower castes.

The interior floor plan displayed a complexity closer to that of an Indian house, with two interior patios surrounded by colonnaded galleries. Each patio had its own function; the first reserved for the owner's family, the second for servants, who could not mix with their masters.

Between the two patios was the *vasary*, or dining room, which stretched the width of the house. It separated the rooms at the front of the house from those of the kitchen area. At one end of this extremely long room, it is still possible to see an elevated platform for musicians, who were an indispensable feature of weddings and family dinners. Because the *vasary* opened onto both patios, without any walls, the three spaces formed a group with multiple perspectives and ever-changing light throughout the day, creating a soft and refined atmosphere worthy of an oriental palace.

Left. *Porch of the main façade and façade of the private chapel of the Casa dos Loyóla Furtado in Orlim.*
Photo H. C.

Previous page. *Elevation and plan of the Casa dos Loyóla Furtado in Orlim.*
Survey by At. H. C.

Right. *Sequence of veranda shutters showing the aesthetic quality and the technical refinement of Indo-Portuguese joinery. Casa dos Loyóla Furtado in Orlim*

While the house's interior decoration has entirely disappeared, the shutters from the reception room windows still bear witness to the refined styles of 19th century Goan joinery.

The superb location of this house, commanding groves of coconut palms and extensive rice fields, gives it a unique environment among the Indo-Portuguese houses we have seen thus far.

The extensive façade is the result of massive, 19th century alteration on a house which probably predated the 18th century. The proportions the house gained during the 19th century reveal, once again, the power and independence that Goan families, particularly Brahmin, acquired during centuries of service in the Portuguese administration.

The coherence in the architectural development of this house over a long period of years reveals as much about the economic and cultural stability of the Goan families as it does about the maintenance of their customs and traditional values. Conceived along the patio house model, this one-storey palace had retained Hindu standards and customs.

In the oldest part of the house, archaic structures appear to date to the early days of Portuguese occupation. This older section is arranged around a central patio, from which one can observe the traditional floor plan. The newer, 19th century wing also has a new interior patio and a second entrance with porch, and acts now as the main part of the house.

The spaces constructed during the 19th century kept the same, traditional functional and symbolic structure, adding only more refinement in the finishing touches and building on a larger scale.

Above. *View of the main façade. Author's drawing*

Previous page. *Porch and ostentatious staircase of the Casa dos Figueiredo in Loutulim*

Above. *Detail of the façade. Casa dos Figueiredo in Loutulim*

With its larger proportions, the newer patio is similar to the old *raj angan* of the Hindu house, with an interior gallery open onto the central outdoor space, improving the circulation of air.

The porch, polarising feature of the façade, is linked to a monumental staircase with enormous columns supporting its roof. The form of this veranda, with a steeply inclined, four-sided roof, reverts to 17th and 18th century porch styles. Even its serpentine-shaped staircase is reminiscent of the baroque period.

The internal floor plan is conceived in traditional fashion, with an entrance in the form of a corridor which ends at a door leading on to the private regions of the house. This door, which according to the Indo-Portuguese model must open onto a patio, opens instead onto a

long and narrow room with the form of an ancient *vasary*. This is more a practical consideration than a disagreement with tradition, for it results from the family's readapting the old wing of the house. As in some large Hindu houses, whose owners had magnificent lifestyles, the *vasary* was doubled in another room, with one for daily use while the other was reserved for special occasions. This separation was required by religious rules on food, with one dining room used for the consumption of vegetarian food and another for food such as fish.

Because it might have to receive guests, the main *vasary* would be placed at the front end of the house, closer to the sitting rooms. In this house, this room runs the length of the new façade, and is kept separate from daily household life.

196

Left. *View of the gardens seen from the entrance porch. Casa dos Figueiredo in Loutulim*

Throughout the house, slatted ceilings are used for air circulation, and early 20th century frescoes cover the walls. The interiors have not received the same attention in finishing touches as has the exterior, but the furniture of the house is very fine indeed, and the pieces collected by the house's last owners constitute a precious collection.

Neo-Gothic XI
and «Fin de Siècle» taste

IN INDO-PORTUGUESE ARCHITECTURE

While Romanticism became a highly-popular decorative fashion in 19th century Indo-Portuguese house, the neo-Gothic style and late 19th century revivals only manifested themselves in the addition of subtle decorative details in an architecture that really owed its heritage to the 18th century.

Goan shipowners and the port of Pangim, while maintaining a fair amount of trade, were gradually relegated to a secondary position as British economic power overwhelmed the Orient. The unchanging forms of Indo-Portuguese architecture reflect growing apathy among their owners.

The neo-Gothic style was introduced to Goa through religious architecture, with the construction or renovation of churches such as Our Lady of Rosário de Saligão in Chandor. In the late 19th century São Pedro church, the façade revived the 16th century Manueline style, albeit with some new decorative details.

In civil architecture, neo-Gothic was seen as being closer to medieval themes: one finds small crenellated towers of military inspiration. The most interesting case is undoubtedly the Casa dos Miranda in Revorá. The porch was converted into a two-storey watch tower, with battlements at its corners. A photograph in the Paul and De Sousa collection shows a group of pavilions belonging to the Counts of Mahém, where the same theme of a turret with battlements may also be seen. In both examples, the turrets are enveloped in large verandas, which give the architecture a colonial touch by emphasising the semi-outdoor spaces.

Above. *Veranda of the Casa dos Cabrais in Nagoa*

Previous page. *View of a reception room and veranda in the Casa dos Quadros e Costa in Loutulim*

199

In the Roldão de Sousa house, there is an interesting neo-Manueline theme in the window frames. Made of stucco, they reproduce an arch design that, curiously enough, is very frequent in the Cochin region. This 16th century style corresponds to the first churches built by the Portuguese for their garrisons in the east. Because of their small size, they have almost completely disappeared through being converted into larger churches with naves.

Alongside some scattered examples where the Manueline and Gothic styles were revived, such as in the Miranda house in Revorá or that of the Counts of Mahém, they appear usually in the small detail of a broken-arch window. But even these windows, whose ornamentation is highly varied, reveal more of a revival of Indo-Portuguese themes than of the older European schools. This broken-arch window ended up by becoming the typical window form on patio houses.

As for interior living spaces, this period brought another modification in taste, but not one that reversed existing aesthetics. The

Above. Pavilion of the now no longer exisiting Casa dos Condes de Mahém over the Mahém lake. Photograph taken at the end of the 19th century. Paul and De Sousa Archives, Pangim

Right. Entrance porch with neo-Gothic decoration similar to that of the Casa dos Condes de Mahém. Photo H. C.

200

individualism of the 19th century incited the creation of an atmosphere of nostalgia, involving the memories of the golden age of the house and its owners. Travel souvenirs, photographs, gifts and an infinite number of decorative bibelots (often of doubtful quality) cropped up in sitting rooms, studies and bedrooms, where formal values were neglected in favour of poetic disorder.

Comforts of a more feminine inspiration appeared: lacework and embroideries multiplied, and often were mingled with memories of long evening parties. Beds, which had been rare during the 18th century, were now more common, and they too attracted the attentions of ladies, who would decorate their canopies with fine lacework, embroidery, fringes and tassels.

Furniture became more varied, both in use as well as form. Tables and dressers multiplied in quantity, covered with objects and souvenirs of the most varied nature.

Chinese influences were still present, as a result of continued trade with Macao. Apart

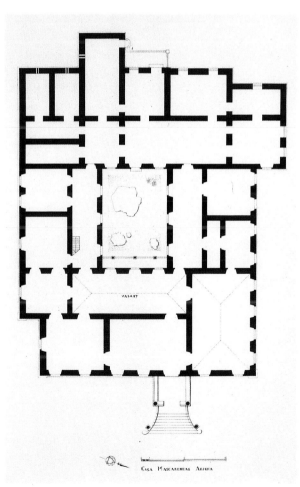

Above. *View of the façade and detail of the porch of the Casa dos Mascarenhas in Anjuna. Drawing and photo by H. C.*

Left. *Plan of the ground floor of the Casa dos Mascarenhas in Anjuna. Survey by At. H. C.*

201

Above and right. *Entrance porch and detail of the family coat of arms of the Mascarenhas in Anjuna*

Following page. *Sequence of reception rooms with 19ᵗʰ century Indo-Portuguese furniture. Casa dos Mascarenhas in Anjuna*

Right. *Room used for occasions of pomp and ceremony. The neo-Gothic late 19ᵗʰ century windows should be noted. Casa dos Mascarenhas in Anjuna*

from a few imports or copies of European
pieces, the furniture was essentially in dark-
coloured, precious woods, with a few rare
cases of upholstered or tapestried chairs and
couches.

A lifestyle made of long conversations in the
shade of verandas, enjoying the evening and
the fresh air at day's end, made this house the
perfect model for the hot, humid climate of
India.

Left. *Large Indo-Portuguese shrine showing Chinese influence. Casa dos Quadros e Costa in Loutulim*

THE CASA DOS QUADROS E COSTA IN LOUTULIM   XI-1

Built at the end of the 19th century, this house belongs to one of the first Brahmin families of Goa to receive the title of Moço-Fidalgo (knight-gentleman) of the royal household. In 1695, António de Quadros received this award[84], and the family was thus able to be, in the eyes of the viceroy, on a par with the noble Portuguese families.

The present house, built by two wealthy priests, Pedro de Alcântura Lamartine de Quadros and Lourenço Avelino Xavier de Quadros[85], was bequeathed, for lack of heirs, to the Costa de Cortorim family.

Rooted for centuries in the Loutulim community, the Quadros owned another, older house, with a large chapel attached to the house, but this one was left to the church, and a religious order now occupies it.

Among the civilian constructions of the late 19th century, this house appears as a variation on the patio house type, still well-adapted to the local climate and to the traditional lifestyle of Goan families.

Without the emphasis of a porch, a veranda stretches around the whole of the façade, and is covered by an extension of the house's roof. In these qualities, it resembles the older houses of the Eucher Pereira and Cabrais families of Nagoa. This house type is a result of a struc-

Above and left. *Main façade over the gardens and detail of column with palm decoration from the veranda of the Casa dos Quadros e Costa in Loutulim. Author's drawing*

[84] **Xavier**, Felipe Nery, *Nobiliarchia Goana*, New Goa, 1862.

[85] **Santo**, Manuel Bruto da Costa Marques dos, and **Costa**, Pedro Miguel do Carmo, *Genealogia da Família Costa de Margão*, vol. I, p. 112.

Above. *Although without its original structure in carved wooden ceiling which acted as a natural system for the circulation of air and airing of the interiors. This ceiling is one of the most beautiful examples of the style typical of Indo-Portuguese interiors*

Following page. *View of the same room with a remarkable settee. Casa dos Quadros e Costa in Loutulim*

tural simplification of rooflines, designed to keep out the rain. The veranda, both very wide and very long, was a favourite spot for relaxing and also served to aerate the house. On the side of the house, another veranda, with columns decorated with carvings of leaves, similar to those at the Cabrais house. The leaf-work coiled around the columns is simpler than that of late 18th century columns, when decorative designs for houses were more closely linked to those for altars, churches and chapels.

Here, however, the size of the columns, and their design resembling palm trees, was of remarkable quality, and emphasised the 19th century leaning towards more naturalistic, Hindu aesthetics. The façade's turquoise blue

colour also had a marvelous optical effect when seen through the dark green trees. Unlike the whitewash favoured by the Portuguese, Indian taste leaned towards naturalist sensitivities, which became more and more fashionable as the 19th century progressed.

Alongside Indian sensibility, which asserted itself with the greatest simplicity during the 19th century, many stylistic references continued to be made to European taste, diffused by the church. The broken-arch design over windows introduced during this period had its origin in the local construction of neo-Gothic parish churches, and the production of Gothic-style altars and church decorations. But these European elements only affected Indian

houses superficially, and did not affect the conceptual structures of Indo-Portuguese house interiors or exteriors.

The Quadros Costa house's interior presents the traditional model, with a patio forming the nucleus and central element in distributing interior space. A long *vasary* parallel to the façade and opening onto the interior patio linked the social and domestic parts of the house.

One of the reception rooms here contains one of the most beautiful and well-preserved carved slatted wooden ceilings for air circulation. The ceiling structure, small rods arranged in trellis fashion, normally meant these ceilings had short lives and required a great deal of maintenance. While most have disappeared, the 19ᵗʰ century innovation of extending the roofline protected this ceiling from the typical infiltrations of monsoon season. This ceiling

dates from the 19ᵗʰ century, but its style shows a much older influence. The application of small carved and gilt wooden flower ornaments denote appreciation for ecclesiastical taste.

In another room there is an enormous shrine or oratory, suggesting that it was commissioned especially or brought over from another house. Chinese influence is dominant here. Pieces of Chinese export porcelain are mounted in a gilded wood altar, in the manner of the famous porcelain and gilt wood ceiling in the house of the Marquess of Abrantes in London.

One of the bedrooms has a bedside table in the same style, incorporating in its front and sides porcelain saucers, indicating that there must have existed more pieces of furniture of this type.

The carving on the wooden shutters is also exquisite, together with the application of small, stylised flowers on the intersections of the

Left. *Detail of a room and colonnade in the service area showing naif decoration with vine leaves. Casa dos Quadros e Costa in Loutulim*

shutter frames. As a result of their exposure to rain, the veranda columns are in bad condition. They formed a sequence of arches in delicate trellis patterns, decorated by the same painted wood carved flowers. This decoration, which substituted for the 17th and 18th century low-relief carving, was used throughout the house, including in the niche-cupboards in the *vasary*.

The main reception room also displays some of this ecclesiastical influence, housing a set of pelmets and mirrors delicately carved with low-relief, vegetal designs of Hindu influence.

The house's façade is rare in Indo-Portuguese civil architecture, as it faces a garden and the drive approaching the house. This layout is a clear reference to the gardens of the *quintas* and palaces belonging to Portuguese nobility as they appeared in the survey of Pangim and Santa Inês regions carried out during the 18th century.

As with so many others, this house is divided today, having undergone alterations which deprived the façade and interior layout of their harmony.

Few residences of the 19th century reached the proportions and richness of decorations of this house-palace. The extremely long original façade, marked nowadays by a double porch, used to have only one large porch. Having reached the height of its importance as a characteristic feature of the Indo-Portuguese house, this porch has two floors and a four-sided roof. The upper floor takes the form of a veranda, serving, thanks to its large size, as a belvedere room used during the long, peaceful Indian evenings. Despite its domination by this enormous porch, the façade is relatively monotonous. Without the pilasters rhythmically alternating with the windows as they had for more than two centuries on other façades,

Above and left. *Main façade and detail of the porch of the Casa dos Loyóla in Chinchinim. Author's drawing*

Previous page. *Colonnade in the ballroom*

of the central entrance, there are vast areas. On one side is a drawing room for receiving guests, balanced on the other side by an unusual ballroom. Curiously, the long *vasary* seems to have disappeared in this house, having been substituted by a dining room without the typical proportions associated with the *vasary*, and without its traditional location and role as the transition zone between the social and service areas.

All the architectural and decorative efforts in this house appear to have been concentrated in the ballroom. Here, the house takes on a truly palatial atmosphere, unparalleled perhaps in all Goan houses. A group of columns frames the room, creating a surrounding gallery which instills an almost musical vibrancy. The ceiling is arched, and higher at the room's center than at the edges.

In a fitting manner, the drawing-room is profusely decorated wiith stucco work and paintings in *fin de siecle* taste.

As a result of dividing the house among various heirs, the drawing-room lost its original furniture. But despite losing a set of arm chairs and couches like those which are so admired in the drawing room of the Bragança Pereira house, this room still evokes the legendary luxury of Indian maharajahs and the magnificence of the Goan Brahmin and Chardo family lifestyles during the 18th and 19th centuries.

this one has a rhymeless effect. The veranda, which stretches along the whole of the façade, appears supported by a group of column trunks opening out in lotus form, exhibiting a great naturalist influence in Indian art and feeling. This naturalist spirit penetrated the window frames on the veranda, creating a type of internal border with carved wooden rosettes, in the style of some Indo-Portuguese furniture.

In keeping with the formal simplicity of the façade, the interior layout remains relatively simple, with two interior patios. On each side

XI-3 THE CASA DOS MIRANDA IN REVORÁ

Above and right. *Details of the façade and interior patio of the Casa dos Miranda in Revorá*

Half abandoned, perhaps as a result of its unusual location, the approach to this enormous house, lost in the Goan interior, has something of the supernatural about it. The turret which constitutes the entrance porch emerges from a landscape of palm trees, emphasising the almost surreal nature of this house, whose origins are difficult to identify.

The house's surreal nature reveals itself again in the columns of the verandas, which stretch out along the façades from the turreted entrance. Painted in strong ochre, these columns are decorated with a bulbous vegetal design, showing a clear affinity with Hindu temples. European Gothic also makes its mark here, in the fan-lights of the veranda doors, which displays small circular windows with coloured glass.

Following page. *Veranda with columns of Hindu influence*

Contrary to its eclectic exterior, the house's interior retains a typical Indo-Portuguese patio house layout.

As in the Casa dos Loyóla Furtado in Orlim, the splendour of this house required a florr plan based on two separate patios. One served the main part of the house, while the other served the kitchen and servants' quarters.

In the main patio, the columns take one a more classical style, with Corinthian inspirations. The gallery opening fully onto this patio stresses Hindu tradition, a tradition which may be seen in architectural details throughout the house.

Contradicting local values, however, there is no room provided with the role of the *vasary*. The dining room appeaers in European rectangular shape, and does not fulfill the role of transition and articulation between the areas reserved for the owners of the house and the areas used by the servants.

Although bereft of furniture and with some rooms showing signs of obvious decay, the ceilings and doors of the reception rooms are still graced with bas-relief decorations which vouch for the quality of the joinery. The carved motifs are even more evident in the niche cupboards in the dinging room. These display foliage with branches and flowers where, amidst Indian and Portuguese influences, the Chinese influence reveals itself yet again.

Following page. *Veranda of the Casa dos Quadros e Costa in Loutulim*

Conclusion XII

By studying the lengthy period of nearly four centuries, and by examining houses over the entire region of Goa, this book has attempted to define the specific identity of Indo-Portuguese architecture within the framework of colonial architectures.

From its origins in the 16th century, until its final period of splendour in the 19th century, a remarkable continuity of characteristics is evident. Maintained, with only small variations throughout the centuries, these characteristics are clear evidence of a profound cultural interchange between two peoples whose aesthetic and spatial concepts were radically different. Starting from a strictly colonial architecture in the 16th century, it is possible to observe, particularly during the 17th and 18th centuries, a progressive cross-influencing of Indian and Portuguese aesthetic tastes. The resulting mixture, through its originality, assumed the name «Indo-Portuguese» architecture.

By analysing stylistic transformations of Indo-Portuguese architecture during the centuries, it was possible to identify a set of permanent characteristics of this architecture.

For a more accurate understanding of this art, it is important to continue studies of different periods, and to survey significant buildings. Sadly, these unique and marvelous buildings are currently undergoing a gradual process of adulteration, and some are falling into a state of complete ruin.

XIII ACKNOWLEDGMENTS

In the first place special thanks go to *Thelma* and *Eurico da Silva* as well as *Habiba* and *Mário Miranda* for the assistance given and for all the efforts made during the contacts with the different owners of the old houses in Goa.

To the Goan families who very kindly opened their doors as though we were members of the family arriving from Lisbon, a special thank you. In this long list I cannot forget the *Pratapsigh Rane* family, the *Monteiros* and *Costa Frias* of Candolim, the *Piedade Costa* of Majorda, the *Mascarenhas* and *Gama Pinto* of Anjuna, the *Miranda* of Margão, the *Eucher Pereira* of Benaulim, the *Mamais* of Pangim, the *Assis Fernandes* of Colva, the *Fernandes* of Chandor, the *Bragança Pereira* and the *Meneses Bragança*, the *Roldão de Sousa* of Velsao, the *Carmo e Costa*, the *Gonçalves* of Guirim, the *Proença*, the *Aleixo Gomes* and the *Campos* of Calangute, the *Abranches* of Verna, the *Machados* of Nagoa, the *Osório Saldanha* of Arossim, the *Loyóla* of Chinchinim, the *Alemão* of Betalbatim, the *Costa Martins* the *Monteiros* and the *Vaz* of Assolna, the *Machados* of Nagoa, the *Walfrido Antão* and *Formazoni Dias* of Betalbatim, the *Pascoal Gomes* and *Sousas* of Siolim, the *Pintos* and the *Rebelo* of Anjuna.

Thanks to *Comander Alpoim Galvão* for the way in which he put at our disposal his collection of paintings with views of Goa, indispensable for the study of the evolution of Indo-Portuguese architecture.

To my former students who accompanied me to India: *Paula Pacheco, Fernanda Pinto Basto, João Nascimento, Paulo Moreira* and *Tito Sampaio* thanks for all their efforts and the way they offered to carry out the architectural surveys and for the difficulties they underwent in Goa.

To the students who patiently carried out the survey drawings of the houses, *Francisca Teixeira da Mota, Suzana Viegas, Sónia, Agostinho Godinho, Pedro Pombo* and *Nelson* go similar thanks.

Finally, thanks go for the assistance in the investigation given by the *Arquivo Histórico Ultramarino, Gabinete de Estudos Históricos de Fortificação e Obras Militares, Sociedade de Geografia de Lisboa, Biblioteca da Ajuda, Arquivo Nacional da Torre do Tombo, Biblioteca Nacional de Lisboa* and *Biblioteca de Pangim*.

Abreu, Miguel Vicente de. *Catálogo dos Secretários de Estado da Índia Portuguesa, desde 1505 até 1866.* New Goa, 1866; *Noção de alguns filhos distintos da Índia Portuguesa.* New Goa, 1866.

Aires Gomes, Júlio. *Biography of Colonel... Aires José Gomes.* Goa, 1993.

Aragáo, A. C. Teixeira de. *Descrição Geral e Histórica das Moedas Cunhadas em Nome dos Reis, Regentes, e Governadores de Portugal.* Lisbon, 1880.

Azeredo, A. E. de Almeida. *As Comunidades de Goa – História das Instituições Antigas.* Lisbon, 1898.

Azevedo, Carlos de. *A Arte de Goa, Damão e Diu.* 2ⁿᵈ edition, Lisbon, 1966.

Barbosa, Duarte. *Livro em que dá relação do que viu e ouviu no Oriente*, 1516. Lisbon, 1946.

Biervillas, Innigo de. *Voyage à la Côte de Malabar*, Paris, 1736.

Boullaiye, François Le Gouz de la. *Les Voyages et Observations du...* Paris, 1653. Transl. in Boletim da Sociedade de Geografia. Nr. 11, Lisbon, 1903.

Bragança Pereira, A. B de. *Etnografia da Índia Portuguesa.* Bastorá, 1940.

Correa, Gaspar. *Lendas da Índia.* 2ⁿᵈ edition, Lisbon, 1858-64, vol. I and II.

Correia, Alberto Carlos G. da Silva. *História da Colonização Portuguesa na Índia.* Lisbon, 1954.

Coutinho, António Xavier G. Pereira. *História da Aventureira Vida de Um Fidalgo Português na Índia.* Oporto, 1941.

Couto, Diogo de. *Da Ásia – Dos feitos que os portugueses...* Lisbon, 1977-88.

Dellon, Dr. C. *Relation d'un Voyage fait aux Indes Orientales.* Amsterdam, 1699; *Narração da Inquisição de Goa.* New Goa, 1866.

Feio, Mariano. *As Castas Hindus de Goa.*

Fonseca, José Nicolau da. *Sketch of The City of Goa.* 2ⁿᵈ edition. New Delhi, 1986.

Forbes, J., *Oriental Memoirs.* London, 1834.

Freyer, John. *East India and Persia.* London, 1909.

Freyre, Padre António. *Primor e Honra da Vida Soldadesca na Índia.* Lisbon, 1630.

Frias, Padre António João de. *Aureola de Indianos. Nobiliarquica Bracmane. Tratado histórico, genealógico, panegírico e moral.* Lisbon, 1702.

Gemelli, Carreri. *Giro delle Mondo*, 9 vol. Venice, 1719. Translated to English in *Churchill's Voyages and Travels*, London, 1834, vol. I.

Grose, Jean Henri. *Voyage aux Indes Orientales.* London, 1753.

Hamilton, Captain Alexander. *A New Account of East Indies.* London, 1744.

Ives, Edward. *A Voyage from England to India.* London, 1773.

Kloguen, Abbé Cottineau de. *An Historical Sketch of Goa.* Madras, 1831, transl. by Cunha Rivara. Instituto Vasco da Gama.

Le Blanc, Vincent. *Les Voyages Fameux du Sieur...*, Paris, 1648.

Linschoten, John Huyghen Van. *The voyage of ... to the East Indies.* New Delhi, 1988, vol. I and II. Lisbon, 1979.

Lopes Mendes A., *A Índia Portuguesa.* Lisbon, 1886.

Lucena. Padre João de. *História da vida do Padre S. Francisco de Xavier...* Lisbon, Officina de António Gomes, 1688.

Mandelslo, Albert de. *The Voyages of ...*, London, 1669.

Memória Histórica-Eclesiástica da Arquidiocese de Goa. Ed. Padre Amaro Pinto Lobo. New Goa, 1933.

Mendonça, Frei J. Gonçalo. *História de las cosas más notables...* Antwerp, 1596.

Miranda, J. C. Barreto. *Memória Descritiva da Villa de Margão.* New Goa, 1859.

O Cronista de Tissuary. Org. by Cunha Rivara. New Goa, 1866.

O Oriente Portugês. New Goa, 1933.

Nazareth, José Maria do Carmo. *Ensaio Descritivo e Estatístico de Pangim.* New Goa, 1865.

Paez, Padre Leonardo de. *Pronptuario das Diffinições Indicas.* Lisbon, 1713.

Parson, Abraham. *Travels in Asia and Africa.* London, 1808.

Pereira, António Pinho. *História da Índia no tempo em que a governou o Vizo-Rey D. Luís de Atayde.* Coimbra, 1617.

Perron, Anquetil du. *Zen Avesta.* Paris, 1771.

Pinto, Celsa. «Goa-Based Overseas and Coastal Trade (18ᵗʰ-19ᵗʰ centuries)» in *Goa Through the Ages.* Goa University, Goa 1989, org. by Teotónio de Souza.

Pinto, Gonçalo Teixeira. *Memórias sobre as Possessões Portuguesas na Ásia.* New Goa, 1859.

Pinto, Maria Helena Mendes. In *Oceanos* «Sentando-se em Goa», nrs. 19-20, 1994.

Pyrard. François de Laval. *Voyage de...* Paris, 1679.

Ramponi, Placido Francesco. *Racconto del Viaggio dell India Orientali e Ocidentali...*, transc. in Garcia de Orta, Lisbon, 1956.

Relação da Viagem que... Fizeram à Índia... os Marqueses de Távora. Lisbon, 1752.

Rego, A. Silva. As Gavetas da Torre do Tombo, Lisbon, C. E. H. U., 1960-77.

Rivara, J. H. da Cunha. *A Conjuração de 1787.* New Goa, Imprensa Nacional, 1875.

Saldanha, Pr. M. J. Gabriel de. *História de Goa*, Vol. II, *Monumentos Arqueológicos*, New Goa. 1926.

Sampayo, João de Melo de. *A Casa dos Melo de Sampaio em Santa Inês.* New Goa, 1904.

Santa Catarina de Siene, Frei Vicenzo Maria di. *Viaggio all India Orientale.* Venice, 1683.

Santos, Manuel Bruto da Costa Marques dos; **Costa**, Pedro Miguel do Carmo. *Genealogia da Família Costa de Margão.*

Sardo, Susana. In *Oceanos* «Goa – Sons e Silêncios», nrs. 19-20, 1994.

Sousa, Padre Francisco de. *Oriente Conquistado.* Lisbon, 1710.

Sousa Viterbo. *Dicionário Histórico e Documental dos Arquitectos.* Imprensa Nacional-Casa da Moeda, Lisbon, 2ⁿᵈ edition, 1988.

Souza, Teotónio R. de. *Goa Medieval – A cidade e o Interior no Século XVII.* Lisbon, Editorial Estampa, 1994.

Tavernier, Jean Baptiste. *Les Six Voyages de...*, Baron d'Aubonne. Paris, 1676.

Valle, Pietro Della. *The Travels of ...in India.* India, Asian Educational Services, 1991.

Visscher, Jacob Canter, *Letters from Malabar.* Translated from the Netherlander by Herber Drury. Madrasta, 1862.

Xavier, Felipe Nery. *Nobiliarchia Goana.* Imprensa Nacional, 1862; *Bosquejo Histórico das Comunidades...* New Goa, 1852.

XV Toponymical Index

CONTENTS

Published in the UK by CARTAGO London
An imprint of KEA Publishing Service Ltd
63 Edith Grove, London SW 10 OLB

First published in Portugal by © 1997 Livros Quetzal S. A.
Text © 1999 Helder Carita
Photographs © 1999 Nicolas Sapieha

The Cataloguing in Publication data for this book
is available from the British Library

Graphic design: Helder Carita
Translated by: Elizabeth Wise

Film, Typesetting and Colour Separation:
Multitipo — Artes Gráficas Lda.

Printed in Portugal by: Printer Portuguesa

info@cartago.net
www.cartago.net

ISBN 1-900826-10-0

Published in the USA by M. T. Train/Scala Books
Distributed by Antique Collectos' Club,
Wappingers Falls, NY 12590